French Word Puzzles

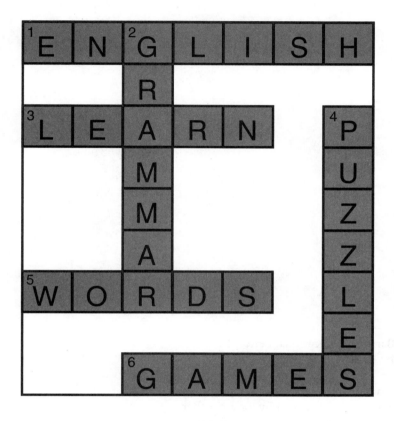

Marcel Danesi, Ph.D.

University of Toronto

BARRON'S

All inquiries should be addressed to:
Barron's Educational Series, Inc.
250 Wireless Boulevard
Hauppauge, New York 11788
http://www.barronseduc.com

ISBN-13: 978-0-7641-3307-7
ISBN-10: 0-7641-3307-1

Printed in the United States of America

9 8 7 6 5 4 3 2 1

Contents

Preface v

EASY PUZZLES 1

Crosswords 1

The House 1
1. Rooms 1
2. At Table 2
3. Furniture 3
4. Objects, Appliances, and Fixtures 4
5. Recreation at Home 6

Word Crosses 7

Family and People 7
6. The Family 7
7. People 8
8. The Body 9
9. Physique 10
10. Personality 11

Scrambled Letters 12

Basic Notions 12
11. Numbers 12
12. Time 12
13. The Weather 13
14. Colors 14
15. Qualities 15

Word Searches 16

Clothing and Footwear 16
16. Clothing 16
17. Footwear 17
18. Jewelry 18
19. Accessories and Things 19
20. Getting Dressed 20

Cryptograms 21

Greetings, Introductions, ... 21
21. Greetings 21
22. Introductions 21
23. Names 21
24. Addresses 22
25. Phoning 22

MODERATE-LEVEL PUZZLES 23

Crosswords 23

Food 23
26. Vegetables 23
27. Fruit 25
28. Meat and Fish 27
29. Bread and Sweets 29
30. Other Foods and Beverages 31

Word Crosses 33

Nouns, Adjectives, and Prepositions 33
31. Noun Plurals 33
32. Adjectives 34
33. Demonstrative Adjectives 34
34. Possessive Adjectives 35
35. Prepositions 36

Scrambled Letters 37

Eating and Drinking 37
36. Drinks 37
37. At the Restaurant 38
38. Let's Eat! 38
39. Descriptions 39
40. Expressions 39

Word Searches 40

Cities, Traffic, and Places 40
41. Cities 40
42. Traffic 41
43. Roads 42
44. Buildings 42
45. Places 43

Cryptograms 44

Politeness and Emotions 44
46. Courtesy 44
47. Politeness 44
48. Anger 44
49. Agreement and Disagreement 45
50. Other Expressions 45

TOUGH PUZZLES 46
Crosswords 46

Jobs and Careers 46
51. Jobs 46
52. Other Jobs 47
53. The Office 48
54. Work Places 49
55. At Work 50

Word Crosses 51

Verbs 51
56. The Present Indicative of Regular Verbs 51
57. Regular and Irregular Past Participles 52
58. The Imperfect of Regular and Irregular Verbs 53
59. The Future of Regular Verbs 54
60. The Conditional of Regular Verbs 55

Scrambled Letters 56

Recreation and Sports 56
61. Sports 56
62. Buildings and Arenas 57
63. Amusement 57
64. Leisure Time 58
65. Recreation 58

Word Searches 59

Health and Emergencies 59
66. At the Hospital 59
67. At the Doctor's 60
68. At the Dentist's 61
69. Ailments 62
70. Emergencies 63

Cryptograms 64

Appearance, Mood, and Intelligence 64
71. At the Beauty Salon 64
72. Cosmetics 64
73. Mood 64
74. Intelligence 65
75. Character 65

CHALLENGING PUZZLES 66
Crosswords 66

Flora and Fauna 66
76. Plants 66
77. Animals 67
78. Birds 69
79. Trees 70
80. Flowers 71

Word Crosses 73

Miscellaneous Grammar Topics 73
81. The Present Indicative of Irregular Verbs 73
82. The Future and Conditional of Irregular Verbs 74
83. Question Structures 75
84. Noun Plurals Again 76
85. Adverbs 77

Scrambled Letters 78

Travel and Transportation 78
86. Cars 78
87. Airports and Airplanes 79
88. Trains and Buses 79
89. Hotels 80
90. Vacations 80

Word Searches 81

Computers and Technology 81
91. Computers 81
92. Television 82
93. Internet 83
94. Communications 84
95. The Phone 85

Cryptograms 86

French Culture 86
96. Writers 86
97. Artists 86
98. Musicians 86
99. Film Directors 87
100. Mathematicians 87

Answers 88

Grammar Charts 103

Word Finder 114

Preface

A good puzzle is its own reward, as the saying goes! Puzzles also have a hidden educational benefit—they can help us learn subjects such as languages easily and efficiently. This book contains a collection of word puzzles designed to help the beginning or intermediate student of French work on the basics of vocabulary and grammar in an enjoyable and effortless way. All you need is a love for solving puzzles. If you are a beginning student, you can use this manual specifically to support and reinforce what you are studying; if you are an intermediate student, you can use this manual instead to brush up and expand your knowledge.

The puzzles cover common topics such as food, clothing, plants, verbs, and French culture. They come in five formats (crosswords, word crosses, scrambled letters, word searches, cryptograms) and increasing levels of difficulty—from easy to challenging. For this reason they are numbered consecutively. As used here, the term "level of difficulty" means that the puzzle clues will become gradually more difficult linguistically as you progress through the book—for example, in the easy and moderate-level sections, you will find that most of the clues are pictures or English equivalents, whereas in the tough and challenging sections, you will find more and more clues that are given only in the French language. Additionally, the solution involves knowing uncommon or unusual vocabulary (names of trees, animals, etc.) or more technical matters.

No matter at what stage of linguistic knowledge you find yourself, you are bound to hit upon specific puzzles that you can solve easily, given the large selection provided—100 in total! The best approach, however, is to try doing them all, starting at the beginning and working your way right through to the most challenging ones. At the end of the book, you will find the answers to all the puzzles and a handy "word finder," which lists the words and expressions (over 1,300 in all!) that you will need to solve the puzzles. Even if you cannot solve some particular puzzle, you will gain linguistically just the same by simply reading its solution. The purpose of this book is, after all, to help you gain proficiency in the French language, not just in puzzle solving. So, do not leave any puzzle half done or completely undone. Try your best to solve each and every one in its entirety. However, if you do get bogged down, look up the answer and finish the puzzle by simply copying the answer. In this way you will ensure that you gain something useful from the puzzle.

The emphasis throughout the book is on vocabulary development. Three grammar word-search sections have been thrown in for good measure (at the moderate, tough, and challenging levels). To help you solve these, there is a Grammar Charts section at the back, which you can consult if you need to brush up on some particular point of grammar.

French Word Puzzles will bring you hours and hours of learning fun, especially if you already know a little French. All you need is a tad of patience and a knack for solving puzzles. *Bonne chance!*

Marcel Danesi
Toronto, 2005

Easy Puzzles

The puzzles in this part are classified as "easy" because the clues given are of the simple variety: pictures and English equivalents. Also, you are given many hints, many more than in any of the remaining parts, including the article form that precedes a noun. Have fun!

CROSSWORDS
The House (La maison)

1. Rooms (Salles)

In this puzzle, the clues are all equivalent English terms referring to rooms or parts of rooms.

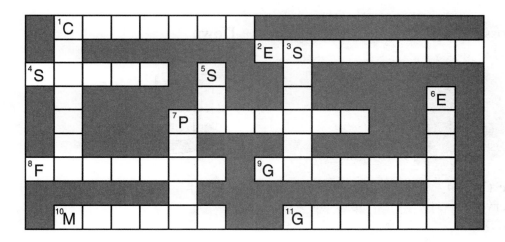

Across
1. kitchen (la ...)
2. stairs (l'...)
4. bathroom (la ... de bains)
7. ceiling (le ...)
8. window (la ...)
9. attic (le ...)
10. dining room (la salle à ...)
11. garage (le ...)

Down
1. bedroom (la ... à coucher)
3. living room (la salle de ...)
5. floor (le ...)
6. entrance (l'...)
7. door (la ...)

2 French Word Puzzles

2. At Table (À table)

The clues are either pictures or equivalent English terms referring to the kinds of things found at table.

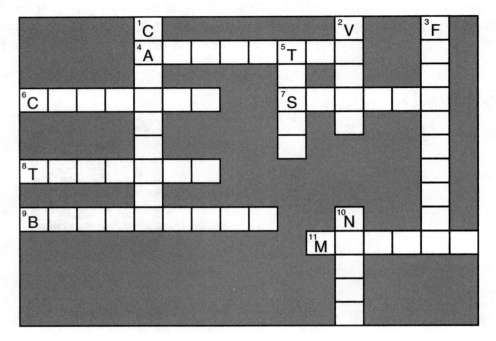

Across

4. (l'...)

6. knife (le ...)
7. to serve
8. (la ...)

9. (la ...)

11. to eat

Down

1. (la ...)

2. (le ...)

3. fork (la ...)
5. (la ...)

10. tablecloth (la ...)

3. Furniture (Les meubles)

The clues are, again, either pictures or equivalent English terms referring to furniture.

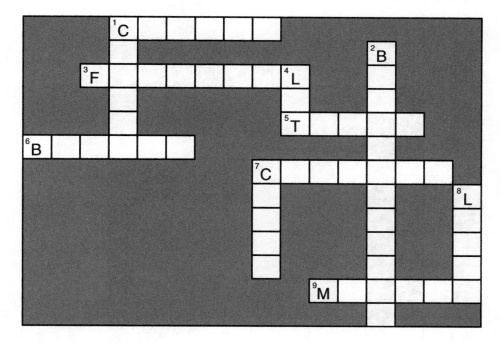

Across

1. (le ...)

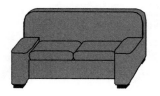

3. (le ...)

5. table (la ...)
6. (le ...)

7. chest of drawers (la ...)
9. piece of furniture (le ...)

Down

1. (la ...)

2. (la ...)

4. (le ...)

7. frame (le ...)
8. lamp (la ...)

4. Objects, Appliances, and Fixtures (Les objets, les appareils et les installations)

The clues are pictures of familiar household things, appliances, or fixtures.

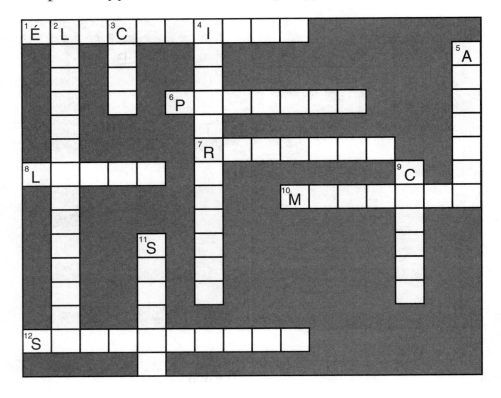

Across
1. (la lampe ...)

6. (la ...)

Down
2. (le ...)

3. (la ...)

Across (continued)	**Down (continued)**

7. (le ...)

4. (l'...)

8. (la machine à ...)

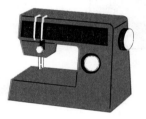

5. (l'...)

10. (la ... à coudre)

9. (le ...)

12. (les ...)

11. (le ...)

5.   Recreation at Home (La récréation domicile)

The clues are, once again, pictures of familiar household things.

Across

1.   (l'... parabolique)

3.   (la ...)

4.   (le ... compact)

5.   (le ...)

6.   (la ... stéréo)

Down

1.   (l'...)

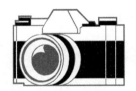

2.   (la ...)

WORD CROSSES

Family and People (La famille et les gens)

The given word in the vertical column of each puzzle is related to the theme of the puzzle.

6. The Family (La famille)

The clues are equivalent English kinship terms.

Clues

1. mother (la ...)
2. grandfather (le ...)
3. aunt (la ...)
4. female cousin (la ...)
5. father (le ...)
6. uncle (l'...)
7. sister (la ...)
8. son (le ...)
9. daughter (la ...)
10. brother (le ...)

7.   People (Les gens)

The clues are, again, equivalent English terms, this time referring to people.

Clues

1. populace, people (le ...)
2. woman (la ...)
3. boy (le ...)
4. friends (les ...)
5. man (l'...)
6. people (les ...)
7. enemy (l'...)
8. girl (la ...)

8. The Body (Le corps)

The clues are pictures of the human body.

Clues

1. (la …)

2. (le …)

3. (le …)

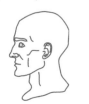

4. (la …)

5. (l'…)

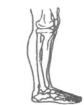

6. (la …)

7. (le …)

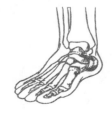

8. (la …)

9. Physique (Le physique)

The clues are equivalent English terms referring to physical traits (tall, short, etc.).

Clues

1. thin, skinny
2. bony
3. fat
4. short
5. muscular
6. athletic
7. tall, big
8. small, short
9. strong
10. weak

10. Personality (La personnalité)

The clues are equivalent English terms referring to personality traits (nice, kind, etc.).

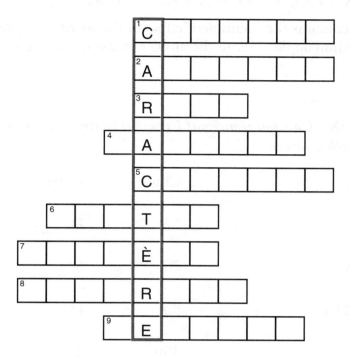

Clues

1. creative
2. kind
3. rude, rough
4. patient
5. cynical

6. nice
7. sincere
8. generous
9. nervous

SCRAMBLED LETTERS
Basic Notions (Les notions élémentaires)

The first column contains the scrambled letters of the word or expression to which the clue in the middle column applies. Write the answer in the third column by unscrambling the letters.

11. Numbers (Les nombres)

Each clue is a number. Can you figure out its verbal equivalent? As a hint, you are given the first letter of each answer.

Scrambled Letters	Clues	Answers
1. OUDZE	12	D _____
2. XANSOITE-IDX	70	S _____
3. TRQUAE-VNGITS	80	Q _____
4. OISTR CNTES	300	T _____
5. NU ERTIS	⅓	U _____
6. LLMIE	1 000	M _____
7. NU MLIOILN	1 000 000	U _____
8. EMIEPRR	1ˢᵗ	P _____
9. ZIÈMQUINE	15th	Q _____
10. NGVIT-TE-IÈUNME	21st	V _____

12. Time (L'heure)

Each clue is a number indicating time of day. What is the equivalent in words of the number? As a hint, you are given, again, the first letter of each answer.

Scrambled Letters	Clues	Answers
1. DIMI	12:00 P.M.	M _____
2. NUIMIT	12:00 A.M.	M _____

3. NEU URHEE INCQ 1:05 U _____

4. NEU EUHRE TE DMIEE 1:30 U _____

5. UXDE UREHES TE UARTQ 2:15 D _____

6. XDI UREHES UD ATMIN 10 A.M. D _____

7. XDI HUERES UD IRSO 10 P.M. D _____

8. XDEU HRESEU ED L'ARÈPS-MDII 2:00 P.M. D _____

13. The Weather (Le temps)

The clues are pictures indicating weather conditions. As a hint, you are given a phrase that accompanies the weather term.

Scrambled Letters	Clues	Answers
1. GEUNUAX		Il est …
2. ERCOUVT		Il est …
3. SLEOIL		Il fait du …
4. VNTE		Il fait du …

5. OIDFR

Il fait …

_____

6. CAUDH

Il fait …

_____

7. EUTPL

Il …

_____

8. IGENE

Il …

_____

14. Colors (Les couleurs)

The clues are equivalent English terms referring to colors. As a hint, you are given the first letter of each answer.

Scrambled Letters	Clues	Answers
1. UGERO	red	R _____
2. LEBU	blue	B _____
3. ERVT	green	V _____

4. UNEJA   yellow   J _____

5. UNBR   brown   B _____

6. VLEIOT   purple   V _____

7. RSEO   pink   R _____

8. BNCLA   white   B _____

9. OIRN   black   N _____

10. ONGERA   orange   O _____

15. Qualities (Les qualités)

The clues are equivalent English terms referring to qualities of things (round, smooth, etc.). As a hint, you are given the first letter of each answer.

Scrambled Letters	Clues	Answers
1. OUXD	sweet	D _____
2. ARME	bitter	A _____
3. DRU	hard	D _____
4. MUO	soft	M _____
5. RNDO	round	R _____
6. SELIS	smooth	L _____
7. OULÉND	wavy	O _____
8. ILLÉMOU	wet	M _____
9. SCE	dry	S _____

WORD SEARCHES
Clothing and Footwear (Les vêtements et les chaussures)

The hidden words can be read in any of three directions: from left to right, from right to left, and top down. Circle them.

16. Clothing (Les vêtements)

The clues are equivalent English terms referring to clothes. As a hint, you are given the number of letters in each hidden word.

A	S	C	P	R	D	S	C	D	C	A	S
C	B	J	U	P	E	Y	H	T	F	R	S
R	Z	A	L	A	S	V	E	S	T	E	M
A	L	D	L	M	L	A	M	S	C	D	C
V	X	N	O	R	A	Z	I	M	M	G	H
A	V	B	V	C	S	A	S	R	T	B	A
T	U	Y	E	B	V	Q	I	O	P	M	P
E	B	O	R	U	C	H	E	M	I	S	E
C	D	A	S	M	L	D	R	A	M	E	A
L	C	D	A	S	M	L	D	A	M	E	U
P	A	N	T	A	L	O	N	R	B	V	A

Clues

1. pants, trousers (letters = 8) (le ...)
2. hat (letters = 7) (le ...)
3. tie (letters = 7) (la ...)
4. jacket (letters = 5) (la ...)
5. shirt (letters = 7) (la ...)
6. blouse (letters = 9) (le ...)
7. skirt (letters = 4) (la ...)
8. dress (letters = 4) (la ...)
9. sweater (letters = 8) (le ...)

17. Footwear (Les chaussures)

The clues are equivalent English terms referring to footwear. As a hint, you are given the number of letters in each hidden word.

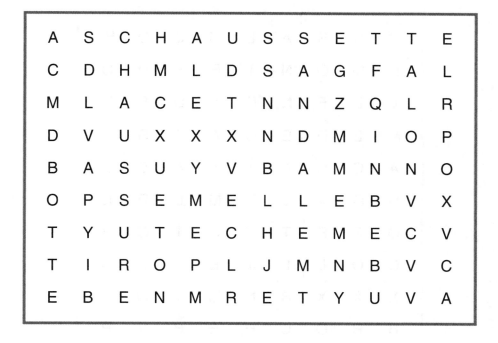

A	S	C	H	A	U	S	S	E	T	T	E
C	D	H	M	L	D	S	A	G	F	A	L
M	L	A	C	E	T	N	N	Z	Q	L	R
D	V	U	X	X	X	N	D	M	I	O	P
B	A	S	U	Y	V	B	A	M	N	N	O
O	P	S	E	M	E	L	L	E	B	V	X
T	Y	U	T	E	C	H	E	M	E	C	V
T	I	R	O	P	L	J	M	N	B	V	C
E	B	E	N	M	R	E	T	Y	U	V	A

Clues

1. boot (letters = 5) (la ...)
2. sock (letters = 10) (la ...)
3. shoe (letters = 9) (la ...)
4. stocking (letters = 3) (le ...)
5. sandal (letters = 7) (la ...)
6. heel (letters = 5) (le ...)
7. sole (letters = 7) (la ...)
8. lace (letters = 5) (le ...)

18. Jewelry (Les bijoux)

The clues are equivalent English terms referring to jewelry. As before, you are given the number of letters in each hidden word.

```
C   D   S   A   L   M   J   O   B
B   M   O   N   T   R   E   U   O
V   L   F   N   C   A   D   S   U
M   L   D   E   C   A   D   S   C
A   C   H   A   Î   N   E   S   L
D   G   V   U   N   M   L   P   E
Q   E   R   T   Y   U   I   O   P
C   O   L   L   I   E   R   B   C
X   X   X   B   N   M   I   O   L
B   R   O   C   H   E   B   V   P
```

Clues

1. watch (letters = 6) (la ...)
2. ring (letters = 6) (l'...)
3. necklace (letters = 7) (le ...)
4. chain (letters = 6) (la ...)
5. earring (letters = 6) (la ...)
6. brooch (letters = 6) (la ...)

19. Accessories and Things (Les accessoires et les choses)

The clues are equivalent English terms for accessories and various other things. As before, you are given the number of letters in each hidden word.

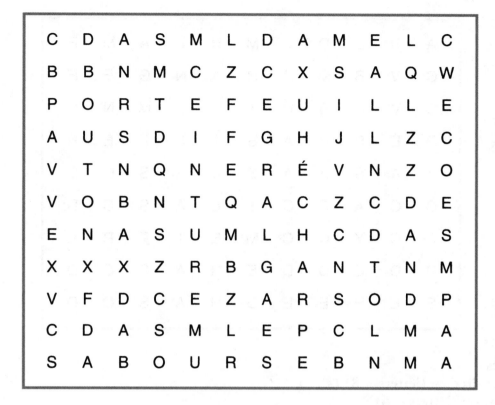

```
C  D  A  S  M  L  D  A  M  E  L  C
B  B  N  M  C  Z  C  X  S  A  Q  W
P  O  R  T  E  F  E  U  I  L  L  E
A  U  S  D  I  F  G  H  J  L  Z  C
V  T  N  Q  N  E  R  É  V  N  Z  O
V  O  B  N  T  Q  A  C  Z  C  D  E
E  N  A  S  U  M  L  H  C  D  A  S
X  X  X  Z  R  B  G  A  N  T  N  M
V  F  D  C  E  Z  A  R  S  O  D  P
C  D  A  S  M  L  E  P  C  L  M  A
S  A  B  O  U  R  S  E  B  N  M  A
```

Clues

1. purse (letters = 6) (la ...)
2. glove (letters = 4) (le ...)
3. scarf (letters = 7) (l' ...)
4. belt (letters = 8) (la ...)
5. button (letters = 6) (le ...)
6. wallet (letters = 12) (le ...)

20. Getting Dressed (S'habiller)

The clues are, again, equivalent English terms referring to dressing. You are also given the number of letters in each hidden word.

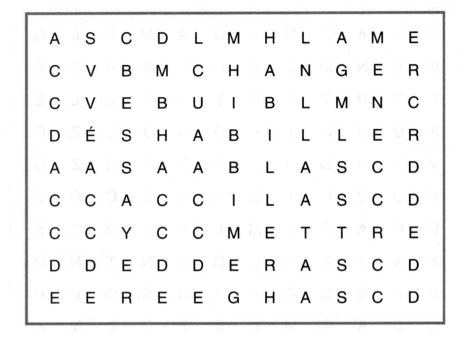

```
A   S   C   D   L   M   H   L   A   M   E
C   V   B   M   C   H   A   N   G   E   R
C   V   E   B   U   I   B   L   M   N   C
D   É   S   H   A   B   I   L   L   E   R
A   A   S   A   A   B   L   A   S   C   D
C   C   A   C   C   I   L   A   S   C   D
C   C   Y   C   C   M   E   T   T   R   E
D   D   E   D   D   E   R   A   S   C   D
E   E   R   E   E   G   H   A   S   C   D
```

Clues
1. to get dressed (letters = 8) (s'...)
2. to put on (letters = 6)
3. to change (letters = 7) (se ...)
4. to get undressed (letters = 11) (se ...)
5. to try on (letters = 7)

CRYPTOGRAMS
Greetings, Introductions, ...
(Les saluts, les présentations, ...)

A specific number will correspond to a specific letter in all the cryptograms. For example, if you establish that 1 = H in any one of the five puzzles, then you can go ahead and substitute H for each occurrence of the digit 1 in the remaining puzzles. The clues for all the puzzles are equivalent English words or expressions.

21. Greetings (Les saluts)

1. Hello!

$$\frac{B}{1}\ \frac{}{2}\ \frac{}{3}\ \frac{}{4}\ \frac{}{2}\ \frac{}{5}\ \frac{}{6}$$

2. Good-bye!

$$\frac{}{7}\ \frac{}{5}\ \ \frac{R}{6}\ \frac{}{8}\ \frac{}{9}\ \frac{}{2}\ \frac{}{10}\ \frac{}{6}$$

22. Introductions (Les présentations)

1. My name is ...

$$\frac{J}{4}\ \frac{}{8}\ \ \frac{}{11}\ '\ \frac{}{7}\ \frac{}{12}\ \frac{}{12}\ \frac{}{8}\ \frac{}{13}\ \frac{}{13}\ \frac{}{8}$$

2. A pleasure!

$$\frac{E}{8}\ \frac{}{3}\ \frac{}{14}\ \frac{}{15}\ \frac{}{7}\ \frac{}{3}\ \frac{}{16}\ \frac{}{8}$$

23. Names (Les noms)

1. given (first) name

$$\frac{}{3}\ \frac{}{2}\ \frac{M}{11}$$

2. surname (family name)

$$\frac{}{3}\ \frac{}{2}\ \frac{}{11}\ \ \frac{}{17}\ \frac{}{8}\ \ \frac{}{18}\ \frac{}{7}\ \frac{}{11}\ \frac{}{10}\ \frac{}{13}\ \frac{}{13}\ \frac{}{8}$$

24. Addresses (Les adresses)

1. street

$$\overline{\quad} \ \overline{\quad} \ \overline{\quad}$$
$$6 \quad 5 \quad 8$$

2. I live at …

$$\overline{\quad} \ \text{,} \quad \overline{\quad} \ \overline{\quad} \ \overline{\quad} \ \overline{\quad} \ \overline{\quad} \ \overline{\quad} \quad \overline{\quad} \ \overline{\quad}$$
$$4 \qquad 15 \ \ 7 \ \ 1 \ \ 10 \ \ 16 \ \ 8 \qquad 7 \ \ 5$$

25. Phoning (Téléphoner)

1. Hello!

$$\overline{\quad} \ \overline{\quad} \ \overline{\quad} \ \overset{\wedge}{\overline{\quad}}$$
$$7 \quad 13 \quad 13 \quad 2$$

2. phone number

$$\overline{\quad} \ \overline{\quad} \ \overline{\quad} \ \overset{,}{\overline{\quad}} \ \overline{\quad} \ \overline{\quad}$$
$$3 \quad 5 \quad 11 \quad 8 \quad 6 \quad 2$$

Moderate-Level Puzzles

The puzzles in this part are a bit harder than the ones in the previous part. The clues are similar. Most are, again, pictures or English equivalents. However, French material is used in the word crosses section. You are given plenty of hints but fewer than in the previous part. You are also given the article form that precedes a noun. Again, have fun!

CROSSWORDS
Food (Les aliments)

26. Vegetables (Les légumes)

In this crossword puzzle, the clues are pictures of various vegetables.

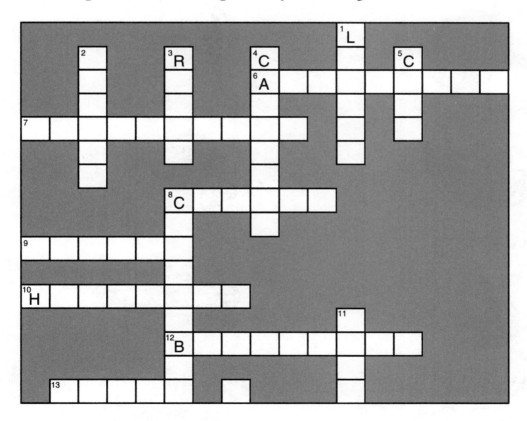

Across	Down
6. (l'...)	1. (la ...)

7. (le ...)   2. (la ...)

8. (le ...)   3. (le ...)

9. (l'...)   4. (les ...)

10. (les ...)   5. (le ...)

12. (la ...)   8. (le ...)

13. (la ... de terre)   11. (le ...)

27. Fruit (La fruit)

The clues are pictures of various fruits.

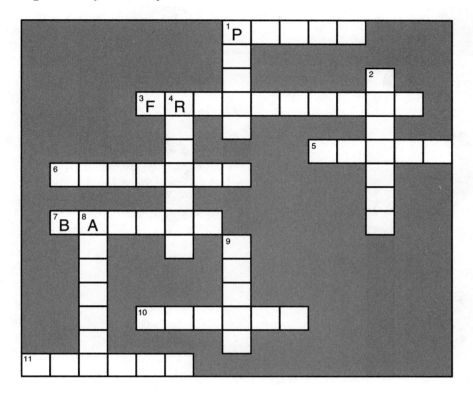

Across	**Down**
1. (la ...)	1. (la ...)

3. (les ...)	2. (les ...)
5. (la ...)	4. (les ...)

Across (continued)	**Down (continued)**

6. (les …)

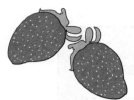

8. (l'…)

7. (la …)

9. (la …)

10. (l'…)

11. (le …)

28. Meat and Fish (Les viandes et les poissons)

The clues are pictures of various meats or fish.

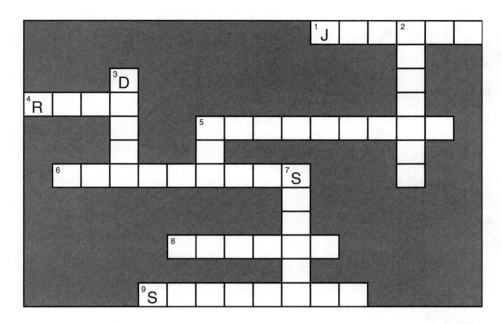

Across	Down
1. (le …)	2. (le …)

   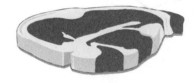

4. (le …)	3. (la …)

5. (le …)	5. (le … dog)

Across (continued)

6. (les …)

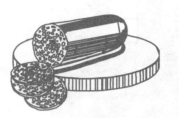

8. (le …)

9. (les …)

Down (continued)

7. (le …)

29. Bread and Sweets (Le pain, les bonbons et les desserts)

The clues are pictures of breads and sweets.

Across

3. (les …)

5. (la …)

Down

1. (le …)

2. (les … pains)

Across (continued)	Down (continued)

Across (continued)

7. (le ...)

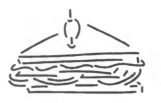

8. (le ...)

9. (le ...)

Down (continued)

3. (le ...)

4. (le ...)

6. (la ...)

30. Other Foods and Beverages (Autres aliments et boissons)

The clues are pictures of various other foods and beverages.

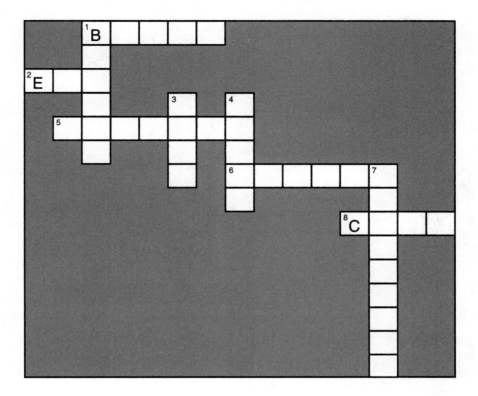

Across

1. (la ...)

2. (l'... minérale)

Down

1. (le ...)

3. (le ...)

Across (continued)	**Down (continued)**
5. (le …)	4. (les …)

6. (les …)

7. (les …)

8. (le …)

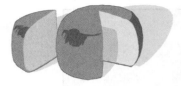

WORD CROSSES

Nouns, Adjectives, and Prepositions
(Les noms, les adjectifs et les prépositions)

The given word in the vertical column of each puzzle is related to the theme of the puzzle. If you have forgotten your French grammar, simply consult the "Grammar Charts" section at the back.

31. Noun Plurals (Le pluriel des noms)

Each clue is the singular form of the required plural noun.

Clues

1. (la) plume
2. (le) lieu
3. (le) bureau
4. (le) cours

5. (le) ciel
6. (le) jeu
7. (le) livre

32. Adjectives (Les adjectifs)

Each clue consists of the masculine form of an adjective. Can you figure out its corresponding feminine form?

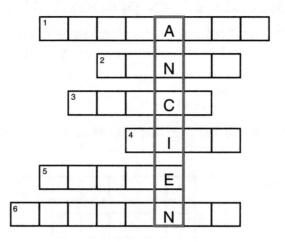

Clues

1. élégant
2. bon
3. doux
4. vif
5. amer
6. ancien

33. Demonstrative Adjectives (Les adjectifs démonstratifs)

Can you figure out which form of the demonstrative adjective is required before each given word in the clues?

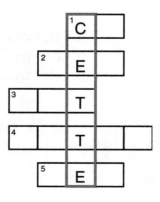

Clues

1. garçon
2. jeux
3. ami
4. amie
5. idées

34. Possessive Adjectives (Les adjectifs possessifs)

Each clue, except the sixth one, gives you the corresponding English possessive adjective. The sixth clue relates to the theme of this puzzle.

Clues

1. his tante
2. their livres
3. her frères
4. your mère

5. my amie
6. possessives (les ...)
7. your ami
8. her oncle

35. Prepositions (Les prépositions)

The clues are equivalent English prepositional phrases.

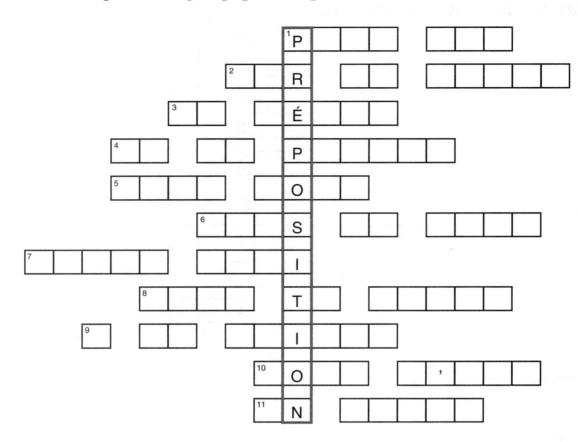

Clues

1. for me
2. on the table
3. in metal (made of metal)
4. of the country
5. (he is living) with us
6. in a month
7. after which
8. with your sister
9. at home
10. under water
11. in winter

SCRAMBLED LETTERS
Eating and Drinking (Manger et boire)

The first column contains the scrambled letters of the word or expression to which the clue in the middle column applies. Unscramble the letters, and write the answer in the third column.

36. Drinks (Les boissons)

The clues are equivalent English terms or expressions referring to drinks and drinking.

Scrambled Letters	Clues	Answers
1. OIRBE	to drink	_____
2. AEU	water	(l') _____
3. IMFA	hunger	(la) _____
4. OISF	thirst	(la) _____
5. À AL SNTAÉ	To your health!	_____
6. NIV	wine	(le) _____
7. BSSOOIN ONN ASCOOLLIÉE	soft drink	(la) _____
8. DLNAIMOE	lemonade (fizzy)	(la) _____
9. NGEORAADE	orangeade	(l') _____

37. At the Restaurant (Au restaurant)

The clues are equivalent English terms that can be used at a restaurant.

Scrambled Letters	Clues	Answers
1. MUEN	menu	(le) _____
2. OURBPOIRE	tip	(le) _____
3. GANRÇO	waiter	(le)
4. SVEUERSE	waitress	(la) _____
5. CANDOMME	order	(la) _____
6. TIONPOR	serving	(la) _____
7. RTIONÉSERVA	reservation	(la) _____

38. Let's Eat! (Mangeons!)

The clues are equivalent English verbs referring to actions that characterize dining.

Scrambled Letters	Clues	Answers
1. NGEMAR	to eat	_____
2. CPEOUR	to cut	_____
3. SNTIER	to taste	_____
4. SEVERR	to pour	_____
5. SRVIER	to serve	_____
6. NDRPREE	to have (something)	_____
7. RVERSENER	to spill	_____

39. Descriptions (Les descriptions)

The clues are equivalent English adjectives that describe how food is prepared or how it tastes.

Scrambled Letters	Clues	Answers
1. ALSÉ	salty	_____
2. ICÉPÉ	spicy	_____
3. UXDO	sweet	_____
4. RILGLÉ	grilled	_____
5. ÔTRI	roasted	_____
6. UA FROU	baked	_____
7. ÛRM	ripe	_____
8. ARIGE	sour	_____

40. Expressions (Les expressions)

The clues are additional equivalent English expressions referring to foods, condiments, and ways of preparing food.

Scrambled Letters	Clues	Answers
1. BENI ITCU	well done	_____
2. NE UCSAE	in a sauce	_____
3. LADSAE ED RUFSIT	fruit salad	_____
4. ORHS D'OEEUVR	appetizer, starter	(l') _____
5. UITFRS ED ERM	seafood	(les) _____
6. PRÉUE ED MMPOES ED TRREE	mashed potatoes	(la) _____

WORD SEARCHES
Cities, Traffic, and Places (Les villes, le trafic et les lieux)

The hidden words can be read in any of three directions: from left to right, from right to left, and top down. Circle them. In each puzzle you are shown where one of the hidden words is.

41. Cities (Les villes et les cités)

The clues are equivalent English terms describing cities and related concepts (suburbs, bridges, etc.).

E	R	T	U	I	B	N	M	L	O	C	S	C
A	D	L	B	H	J	C	A	D	S	G	R	A
A	D	L	A	H	J	C	A	D	S	G	R	P
A	D	L	N	H	J	C	A	D	S	É	S	I
B	A	N	L	I	E	U	S	A	R	D	S	T
A	D	L	I	H	J	C	A	D	S	I	S	A
E	R	T	E	H	J	C	A	D	S	F	S	L
A	D	L	U	H	J	C	A	D	S	I	A	E
A	D	L	E	H	J	C	A	D	S	C	H	J
A	D	L	E	U	P	O	N	T	A	E	H	J
E	R	T	U	I	B	N	M	L	O	C	S	A
E	U	E	L	L	I	V	N	M	L	O	C	S

Clues

1. building
2. bridge
3. capital city
4. suburbs
5. suburbanite
6. downtown, city center

42. Traffic (Le trafic et la circulation)

The clues are pictures or equivalent English words referring to traffic and getting around.

H	E	U	R	E	S	S	A	P
C	D	A	S	M	L	D	E	A
L	D	C	F	C	A	D	S	R
C	É	D	E	R	L	D	E	C
B	P	B	U	U	A	D	S	M
N	A	N	I	E	U	O	S	È
M	S	M	P	A	R	R	Ê	T
L	S	L	C	A	D	S	D	R
P	E	P	C	A	D	S	D	E
A	R	A	C	A	D	S	D	A

Clues

1. (le ... de signalisation)

2. (... le passage)

3. (le ...)

4. (l'...)

5. to pass
6. rush hour (... de pointe)

43. Roads (Les routes)

The clues are equivalent English terms referring to roads and related structures.

```
C  A  D  S  D  M  L  D  E  L  C  A  C
C  A  D  S  D  M  L  D  E  L  C  A  R
R  O  U  T  E  R  R  R  R  G  A  A  O
B  P  H  R  R  F  F  F  F  R  S  S  I
B  P  H  O  T  J  J  J  J  A  D  D  S
S  O  U  T  E  R  R  A  I  N  M  M  E
B  P  H  T  D  M  L  D  E  D  L  L  M
M  L  D  O  T  J  J  J  J  E  E  E  E
B  P  H  I  D  M  L  D  E  M  R  R  N
M  L  D  R  T  J  J  J  J  L  G  G  T
L  D  E  R  U  E  L  L  E  E  T  T  H
```

Clues

1. road (la ...)
2. alley (la ...)
3. intersection (le ...)
4. sidewalk (le ...)
5. underpass (le passage ...)
6. highway (la ... route)

44. Buildings (Les édifices et les bâtiments)

The clues are equivalent English terms referring to buildings.

```
É  G  L  I  S  E  T  Y  U  I  O  P  S
A  D  F  G  H  J  L  O  I  T  C  Z  T
T  R  I  B  U  N  A  L  I  T  C  Z  A
A  D  F  G  H  J  L  O  I  T  C  Z  D
M  U  S  É  E  I  T  C  Z  G  A  R  E
A  D  F  G  H  J  L  O  I  T  C  Z  D
B  I  B  L  I  O  T  H  È  Q  U  E  R
```

Clues

1. church (l'…)
2. museum (le …)
3. library (la …)

4. courthouse (le …)
5. stadium (le …)
6. train station (la …)

45. Places (Les lieux)

The clues are equivalent English terms referring to places.

A	D	G	C	H	U	I	O	P	S	D	B
A	D	G	E	S	D	B	A	S	D	B	A
H	U	I	N	S	D	B	A	R	M	A	R
I	O	P	T	P	S	D	B	E	A	B	E
R	J	A	R	D	I	N	A	S	I	A	S
I	O	P	E	P	S	D	B	D	R	B	D
H	U	I	P	S	D	B	S	C	I	S	C
I	O	P	P	S	D	B	D	B	E	D	B
Q	U	A	R	T	I	E	R	S	D	B	A
H	U	I	O	P	S	D	B	A	Z	O	O

Clues

1. park (le … public)
2. shopping mall (le … commercial)
3. district (le …)

4. city hall (la …)
5. zoo (le …)

CRYPTOGRAMS
Politeness and Emotions
(La politesse, les émotions et les sentiments)

A specific number will correspond to a specific letter in all the cryptograms. For example, if you establish that 1 = H in any one of the five puzzles, then you can go ahead and substitute H for each occurrence of the digit 1 in the remaining puzzles. The clues for all the puzzles are equivalent English expressions.

46. Courtesy (La courtoisie)

1. Thank you! $\frac{M}{1}$ $\frac{}{2}$ $\frac{}{3}$ $\frac{}{4}$ $\frac{}{5}$

2. Welcome! (f.) $\frac{B}{6}$ $\frac{}{5}$ $\frac{}{2}$ $\frac{}{7}$ $\frac{}{8}$ $\frac{}{2}$ $\frac{}{7}$ $\frac{}{9}$ $\frac{}{2}$

47. Politeness (La politesse)

1. Excuse me! $\frac{}{2}$ $\frac{X}{10}$ $\frac{}{4}$ $\frac{}{9}$ $\frac{}{11}$ $\frac{}{2}$ $\frac{}{12}$ - $\frac{}{1}$ $\frac{}{13}$ $\frac{}{5}$

2. Please! $\frac{}{11}$ ' $\frac{}{5}$ $\frac{}{14}$ $\frac{}{8}$ $\frac{}{13}$ $\frac{}{9}$ $\frac{}{11}$

   $\frac{}{15}$ $\frac{}{14}$ $\frac{}{16}$ $\frac{}{5}$ $\frac{}{17}$

48. Anger (La colère)

1. It's Impossible! $\frac{}{4}$ ' $\frac{}{2}$ $\frac{}{11}$ $\frac{}{17}$ $\frac{}{5}$ $\frac{}{1}$ $\frac{}{15}$ $\frac{}{13}$ $\frac{}{11}$ $\frac{}{11}$ $\frac{}{5}$ $\frac{}{6}$ $\frac{}{14}$ $\frac{}{2}$

2. It's not true that ...! $\frac{}{4}$ ' $\frac{}{2}$ $\frac{}{11}$ $\frac{}{17}$ $\frac{}{18}$ $\frac{}{16}$ $\frac{}{9}$ $\frac{}{10}$ $\frac{}{19}$ $\frac{}{9}$ $\frac{}{2}$

49. Agreement and Disagreement (L'accord et le désaccord)

1. Certainly!

$\overline{4}$ $\overline{2}$ $\overline{3}$ $\overline{17}$ $\overline{16}$ $\overline{5}$ $\overline{7}$ $\overline{2}$ $\overline{1}$ $\overline{2}$ $\overline{7}$ $\overline{17}$

2. I disagree!

$\overline{20}$ $\overline{\underset{2}{E}}$ $\overline{7}$ $\overline{2}$ $\overline{11}$ $\overline{9}$ $\overline{5}$ $\overline{11}$

$\overline{15}$ $\overline{16}$ $\overline{11}$ $\overline{21}$, $\overline{16}$ $\overline{4}$ $\overline{4}$ $\overline{13}$ $\overline{3}$ $\overline{21}$

50. Other Expressions (Autres expressions)

1. OK!

$\overline{21}$ ' $\overline{16}$ $\overline{4}$ $\overline{4}$ $\overline{13}$ $\overline{3}$ $\overline{21}$

2. Maybe!

$\overline{15}$ $\overline{2}$ $\overline{9}$ $\overline{17}$ - $\overline{2}$ $\overset{\wedge}{\overline{17}}$ $\overline{3}$ $\overline{2}$

Tough Puzzles

The puzzles in this part are harder than the ones in the previous two parts because most of the clues given to solve the puzzles are in French. You may thus have to look certain things up in a dictionary. There are also fewer hints here than in previous parts, and you are not given the article forms in front of nouns. As always, have fun!

CROSSWORDS

Jobs and Careers
(Le travail et les carrières)

51. Jobs (Le travail)

Each clue consists of a sentence from which the word for a job or profession is missing. Can you figure out what word it is?

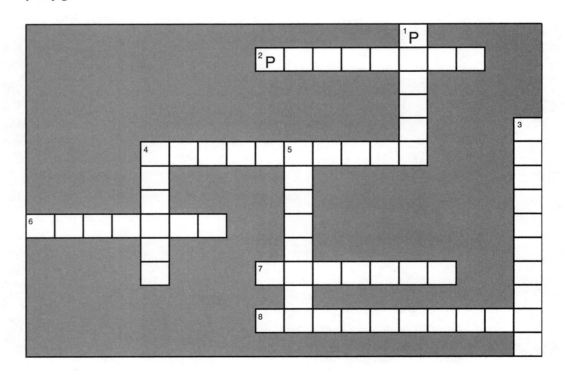

Across

2. Le … a réparé les toilettes.
4. Elle est l'… qui a dessiné ma maison.
6. Il est notre … de famille.
7. Ce … cultive beaucoup de plantes.
8. Mon ami est … à l'université.

Down

1. Ma cousine est … d'avion.
3. Ma soeur est …; elle travaille dans l'hôpital tout près.
4. Mon frère est … de la défense.
5. Comment s'appelle le … qui travaille dans ce magasin d'habillement?

52. Other Jobs (Autres emplois)

Each clue consists of a phrase that indicates what the person does.

Across

1. personne qui joue du piano, par exemple
5. personne qui conduit l'autobus, par exemple
6. personne qui coupe les cheveux
7. personne qui travaille dans un bureau

Down

2. personne qui tient les comptes
3. médecin qui soigne les dentes
4. personne qui travaille "avec l'electricité"
5. personne qui construit les maisons

53. The Office (Le bureau)

The clues are either pictures or descriptions of things found in an office.

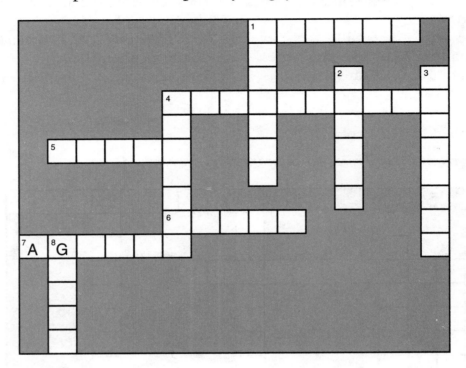

Across

1. Il permet d'écrire.
4.

5.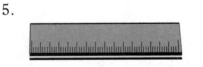

6.

7. Elle permet d'attacher les feuilles.

Down

1. Ils permettent de couper le papier.
2.

3.

4.

8. Elle permet d'effacer.

54. Work Places (Les lieux de travail)

The clues are questions that will ask you where people work (office, store, farm, company, etc.).

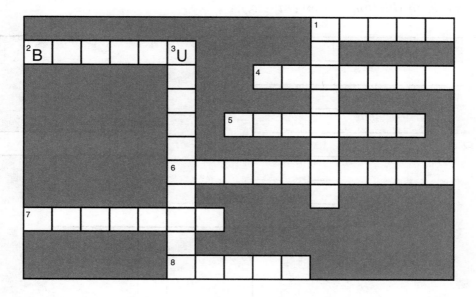

Across	Down
1. Où travaille le fermier?	1. Où travaille l'ouvrier?
2. Où travaille un employé?	3. Où travaille le professeur?
4. Où travaille le médecin?	
5. Où travaille un employé qualifié?	
6. Où travaille le garçon?	
7. Où travaille un vendeur?	
8. Où travaille l'instituteur?	

55. At Work (Au travail)

The clues are near synonyms, descriptive phrases, or characterizations of concepts or activities related to working (hiring, retirement, etc.).

Across
2. congédier
3. terminer de travailler
4. travail
6. entreprendre une activité rémunéré
7. rémunération

Down
1. association de travailleurs
4. prendre quelqu'un au travail
5. pause pour boire le café

WORD CROSSES

Verbs (Les verbes)

The given word in the vertical column of each puzzle is related to the theme of the puzzle. If you have forgotten your French verbs, simply consult the Grammar Charts section at the back.

56. The Present Indicative of Regular Verbs
(Le présent de l'indicatif des verbes réguliers)

Each clue consists of a French infinitive and a pronoun. The latter indicates the present indicative form you are required to figure out. If you know your present indicative conjugations, this puzzle will not be so tough after all.

Clues

1. (aimer) j'...
2. (attendre) tu ...
3. (dormir) elle ...
4. (finir) ils ...
5. (recevoir) nous ...
6. (regarder) vous ...
7. (sortir) ils ...
8. (choisir) je ...
9. (finir) il ...

57. Regular and Irregular Past Participles
(Participes passés réguliers et irréguliers)

Each clue consists of a verb in its infinitive form. Again, if you know your past participles, this puzzle will not be so tough after all.

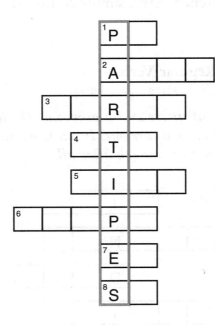

Clues
1. pouvoir
2. aimer
3. dormir
4. être

5. finir
6. romper
7. avoir
8. savoir

58. The Imperfect of Regular and Irregular Verbs
(L'imparfait des verbes réguliers et irréguliers)

Each clue consists of a French infinitive and a pronoun. The latter indicates the imperfect indicative form you are required to figure out. If you know your imperfect conjugations, this puzzle is hardly a tough one for you.

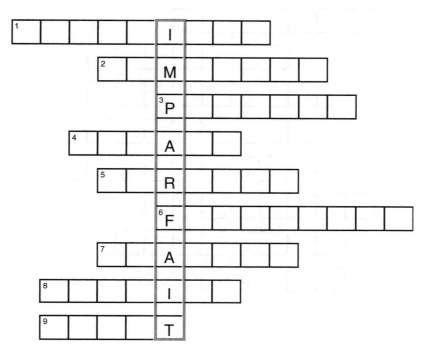

Clues

1. (servir) ils ...
2. (rompre) nous ...
3. (pouvoir) il ...
4. (devoir) elle ...
5. (partir) je ...
6. (finir) tu ...
7. (être) elles ...
8. (donner) vous ...
9. (avoir) il ...

59. The Future of Regular Verbs (Le futur des verbes réguliers)

Each clue consists of a French infinitive and a pronoun. The latter indicates the future form you are required to figure out. As before, if you know your future conjugations, this puzzle is certainly not going to be a tough one to solve.

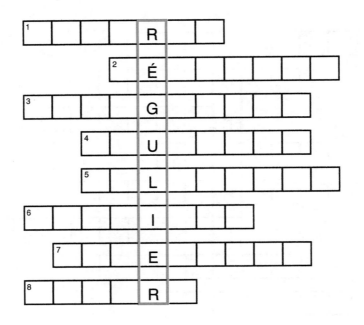

Clues

1. (aimer) je ...
2. (réussir) il ...
3. (changer) nous ...
4. (rougir) tu ...
5. (colorer) vous ...
6. (dormir) je ...
7. (recevoir) ils ...
8. (vendre) elle ...

60. The Conditional of Regular Verbs (Le conditionnel des verbes réguliers)

Each clue consists of a French infinitive and a pronoun. The latter indicates the conditional form you are required to figure out. As with the previous puzzles in this section, if you know your conditional conjugations this puzzle is hardly going to be a "tough" one for you to solve.

Clues

1. (acheter) j'...
2. (répondre) ils ...
3. (finir) tu ...
4. (regarder) vous ...
5. (couvrir) nous ...
6. (partir) elle ...
7. (perdre) tu ...
8. (dormir) je ...
9. (vendre) nous ...

SCRAMBLED LETTERS

Recreation and Sports (La récréation et les sports)

The first column contains the scrambled letters of the word or expression to which the clue in the middle column applies. Unscramble the letters to find the answer, and write it in the third column.

61. Sports (Les sports)

Each clue contains information about the sport.

Scrambled Letters	Clues	Answers
1. ASBE-ABLL	le sport des *Chicago Cubs*	_____
2. OTBFOALL AMAIÉRICN	le sport des *Green Bay Packers*	_____
3. KEBAST	le sport des *Milwaukee Bucs*	_____
4. TNNIES	le sport des soeurs Williams	_____
5. CKEHOY	le sport pratiqué par Wayne Gretzky	_____
6. OTBALFOL	le sport pratiqué par Zidane en France	_____
7. OLGF	le sport pratiqué par Tiger Woods	_____
8. GNASTIQUYME	le sport pratiqué dans le gymnase	_____
9. KSI	le sport pratiqué sur la neige	_____

62. Buildings and Arenas (Les bâtiments et les arènes)

Each clue contains information about a building or arena.

Scrambled Letters	Clues	Answers
1. PINOIRATE	où a lieu un match de hockey	_____
2. ADSTE	où a lieu un match de football	_____
3. CUROT	où a lieu un match de tennis	_____
4. RAITERN	où on joue au football, au base-ball, etc.	_____
5. NASGYME	où a lieu la gymnastique	_____
6. STPIE	où a lieu le ski	_____

63. Amusement (Les distractions)

Each clue describes what is involved in a game or amusement.

Scrambled Letters	Clues	Answers
1. EJU ED DMEAS	le jeu de douze pions noirs et douze rouges	_____
2. ÉHECCS	le jeu caractérisé par l'échec et mat	_____
3. EJU UXA CRTEAS	le poker, par exemple	_____
4. OTMS COISÉRS	le jeu des mots	_____
5. PZZULE	dans ce jeu il faut assembler des éléments pour reconstituer un dessin	_____

64. Leisure Time (Temps libre)

Each clue either describes a type of activity that one can engage in to enjoy leisure time (shopping, going to the movies, etc.) or where it can take place.

Scrambled Letters	Clues	Answers
1. IREFA SDE CRSEOUS	cette activité a lieu dans un centre commercial, par exemple	_____
2. ALELR UA CNÉMIA	cette activité a lieu dans un "cinéplex", par exemple	_____
3. PSSEA-TMPES	une activité très agréable	_____
4. LCTUERE	l'activité de lire	_____
5. AIRFE NUE DPOMENARE	une activité très salutaire	_____
6. ALELR GENAR	cette activité a lieu dans une piscine, par exemple	_____

65. Recreation (La récréation)

Each clue describes what the recreational activity involves (vacationing, holidays, etc.).

Scrambled Letters	Clues	Answers
1. AFRIE UD CMPIANG	les vacances à la campagne	_____
2. VCANACES	une période de "liberté"	_____
3. PNDRREE ED L'EXRCICEE	une activité physique agréable	_____
4. JUEOR UXA ORTSPS	jouer au football, ou base-ball, par exemple	_____
5. AIRFE UD JGINOGG	course à pied faite par exercice	_____

WORD SEARCHES
Health and Emergencies (La santé et les cas d'urgence)

The hidden words can be read in either of two directions: from left to right or top down. Circle the words.

66. At the Hospital (À l'hôpital)

The clues are descriptions of places or activities related to hospitals.

A	O	R	U	R	G	E	N	C	E	H	U	A
S	P	A	S	D	C	M	L	G	H	J	I	M
R	É	A	N	I	M	A	T	I	O	N	B	B
A	R	A	S	D	C	M	L	G	H	J	I	U
M	A	T	E	R	N	I	T	É	M	L	E	L
C	T	A	S	D	C	M	L	G	H	J	I	A
A	I	A	S	D	C	M	L	G	H	J	I	N
D	O	O	U	S	A	L	L	E	P	H	D	C
S	N	A	S	D	C	M	L	G	H	J	I	E

Clues

1. pièce où reposent les malades
2. salle où les maladies sont très graves
3. intervention chirurgicale
4. service hospitalier réservé à les femmes
5. véhicule aménagé pour le transport des malades dans l'hôpital
6. service où les malades ou les blessés reçoivent traitement immédiat

67. At the Doctor's (Chez le médecin)

The clues are synonyms or descriptions of physical states or problems (headache, pain, etc.).

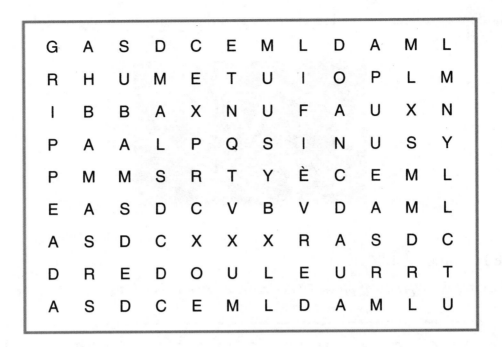

G A S D C E M L D A M L
R H U M E T U I O P L M
I B B A X N U F A U X N
P A A L P Q S I N U S Y
P M M S R T Y È C E M L
E A S D C V B V D A M L
A S D C X X X R A S D C
D R E D O U L E U R R T
A S D C E M L D A M L U

Clues

1. élévation anormale de la température du corps
2. sensation pénible
3. souffrance dans la tête (... de tête)
4. cavité nasale irrégulière
5. inflammation du nez, de la gorge et des bronches
6. maladie contagieuse

68. At the Dentist's (Chez le dentiste)

The clues are synonyms or descriptions of dental devices and problems (cavity, filling, etc.).

C	A	D	S	R	E	Q	C	A	V	I	T	É
Z	V	B	N	M	L	P	A	N	M	I	O	T
Z	V	B	N	M	L	P	R	N	M	I	O	T
C	A	D	S	R	L	V	I	C	A	D	S	R
P	L	O	M	B	A	G	E	N	M	I	O	T
N	M	I	O	T	V	C	A	D	S	R	X	P
C	X	S	A	D	E	N	T	I	E	R	X	O
C	A	D	S	R	R	N	M	I	O	T	X	I
C	A	D	S	R	E	Q	D	S	R	E	U	U

Clues

1. espace vide à l'intérieur d'une cavité dentaire.
2. remplissage d'une cavité
3. maladie des dents
4. nettoyer les dents (se ...)
5. appareil que l'on porte dans la bouche

69. Ailments (Les maladies et les malaises)

The clues are synonyms or descriptions of ailments (cough, nausea, etc.).

```
G  T  I  O  U  V  E  R  T  I  G  E  S  Y
E  R  N  G  T  I  O  U  G  T  I  O  U  Y
O  K  A  G  T  I  O  U  G  T  I  O  U  Y
T  O  U  S  S  E  R  N  M  L  O  U  G  B
E  R  S  G  T  I  O  U  G  T  I  O  U  Y
O  K  E  G  T  I  O  U  G  T  I  O  U  Y
E  R  É  T  E  R  N  U  E  R  O  U  G  B
O  K  B  G  T  I  O  U  G  T  I  O  U  Y
A  L  L  E  R  G  I  E  G  T  I  O  U  Y
```

Clues

1. avoir la toux
2. impression de mouvement circulaire
3. envie de vomir
4. elle est souvent provoquée par les pollens
5. faire une expiration brusque par le nez

70. Emergencies (Les cas d'urgence)

The clues are descriptions of emergency situations or people involved in them (thief, police, etc.).

```
B  A  D  S  C  R  E  T  P  A  M  B  A
B  A  D  S  C  R  E  T  O  S  L  B  G
A  A  A  A  S  V  A  S  M  C  E  A  R
S  S  S  C  D  O  C  D  P  D  L  S  E
D  D  D  P  O  L  I  C  I  E  R  D  S
C  C  C  A  S  E  A  S  E  R  E  C  S
M  M  M  C  D  U  C  D  R  D  F  M  E
L  L  L  N  M  R  V  H  J  L  O  L  U
B  A  D  S  C  R  E  T  J  L  O  B  R
A  U  X  I  L  I  A  I  R  E  N  M  L
B  A  D  S  C  R  E  T  R  E  T  J  L
```

Clues
1. personne qui commet des délits
2. personne qui mantient l'ordre public
3. personne qui combat les incendies
4. personne qui aide les médecins (... médicale)
5. personne qui attaque quelqu'un

CRYPTOGRAMS

Appearance, Mood, and Intelligence
(L'apparence, l'humeur et l'intelligence)

A specific number will correspond to a specific letter in all the cryptograms. For example, if you establish that 1 = H in any one of the five puzzles, then you can go ahead and substitute H for each occurrence of the digit 1 in the remaining puzzles. The clues for the puzzles are synonyms, near synonyms, or descriptions.

71. At the Beauty Salon (Chez l'institut de beauté)

1. C'est une raison pour aller chez le coiffeur.

$$\frac{C}{1} \ \frac{}{2} \ \frac{}{3} \ \frac{}{4} \ \frac{}{5} \qquad \frac{}{6} \ \frac{}{5}$$

$$\frac{}{1} \ \frac{}{7} \ \frac{}{5} \ \frac{}{8} \ \frac{}{5} \ \frac{}{3} \ \frac{}{9}$$

2. C'est une raison pour aller chez l'institut de beauté.

$$\frac{}{4} \ \frac{E}{5} \ \frac{}{10} \ \frac{}{11} \ \frac{}{12} \ \frac{}{13} \ \frac{}{5} \ \frac{}{13} \ \frac{}{14} \ \frac{}{5}$$

72. Cosmetics (Les cosmétiques, les produits de beauté)

1. Il s'applique sur les ongles.

$$\frac{}{8} \ \frac{}{5} \ \frac{}{10} \ \frac{}{13} \ \frac{}{15} \ \frac{}{16} \qquad \frac{}{12} \qquad \frac{}{2} \ \frac{}{13} \ \frac{}{17} \ \frac{}{18} \ \frac{}{5} \ \frac{}{16}$$

2. Il s'applique sur le visage.

$$\frac{}{11} \ \frac{}{12} \ \frac{}{19} \ \frac{}{3} \ \frac{}{15} \ \frac{}{18} \ \frac{}{18} \ \frac{}{12} \ \frac{}{17} \ \frac{}{5}$$

73. Mood (L'humeur)

1. joie

$$\frac{}{20} \ \frac{}{2} \ \frac{}{13} \ \frac{}{7} \ \frac{}{5} \ \frac{}{3} \ \frac{}{10}$$

2. chagrin

$$\frac{}{14} \ \frac{}{10} \ \frac{}{15} \ \frac{}{16} \ \frac{}{14} \ \frac{}{5} \ \frac{}{16} \ \frac{}{16} \ \frac{}{5}$$

74. Intelligence (L'intelligence)

1. créativité

$\overline{15}$ $\overline{11}$ $\overline{12}$ $\overline{17}$ $\overline{15}$ $\overline{13}$ $\overline{12}$ $\overline{14}$ $\overline{15}$ $\overline{2}$ $\overline{13}$

2. stupidité

$\overline{20}$ $\overset{\wedge}{\overline{5}}$ $\overline{14}$ $\overline{15}$ $\overline{16}$ $\overline{5}$

75. Character (Le caractère)

1. personne qui manque
d'égards

$\overline{5}$ $\overline{17}$ $\overline{2}$ $\overline{15}$ $\overline{16}$ $\overline{14}$ $\overline{5}$

2. quelqu'un qui est genereux
et qui agit sans penser à lui-même

$\overline{12}$ $\overline{18}$ $\overline{14}$ $\overline{10}$ $\overline{3}$ $\overline{15}$ $\overline{16}$ $\overline{14}$ $\overline{5}$

Challenging Puzzles

The puzzles in this part are the hardest in this book but certainly not impossible to do. The clues require a little more effort and maybe a trip to the dictionary. You are not given any hints whatsoever. You are on your own. As always, have fun!

CROSSWORDS

Flora and Fauna
(La flore et la faune)

76. Plants (Les plantes)

The clues are descriptions or illustrations of types of plants or plant components (flowers, roots, etc.).

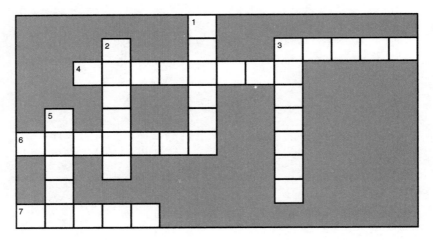

Across
3. une rose, une tulipe et une marguerite, par exemple
4. une herbe "pas bonne"
6. composant d'un arbre, par exemple
7. construction "en verre" où l'on met les plantes

Down
1. "l'origine" d'une plante
2. composant essentiel d'une plante
3. elle est généralement verte
5. plante avec des branches et des feuilles

77. Animals (Les animaux)

Do you recognize the following animals? Can you name them in French? Unless you are an animal lover, this is truly a challenging puzzle. Good luck!

Across	Down

2.

6.

1.

3.

Across (continued)

7.

8.

9.

11.

14.

15.

Down (continued)

4.

5.

9.

10.

12.

13.

78. Birds (Les oiseaux)

Do you recognize the following birds? Can you name them in French? Again, unless you are a bird lover, this is truly a challenging puzzle. Good luck!

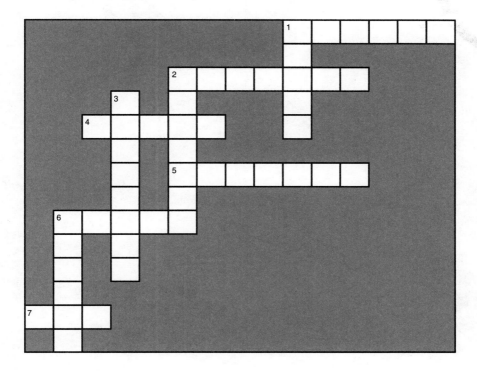

Across

1.

2.

4.

Down

1.

2.

3.

Across (continued)   **Down (continued)**

5.      6.

6.

7.

79. Trees (Les arbres)

The clues are all descriptions of various trees.

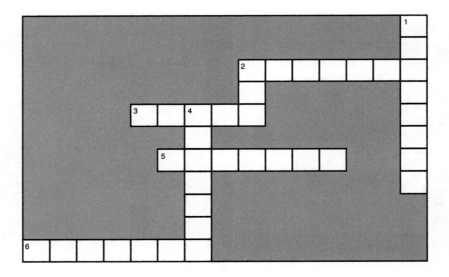

Across
2. l'arbre qui produit des pommes
3. l'arbre de Noël
5. l'arbre qui produit des olives
6. l'arbre qui produit des poires

Down
1. l'arbre qui produit des cerises
2. l'arbre qui produit des aiguilles
4. l'arbre avec des palmes

80. Flowers (Les fleurs)

Do you recognize the following flowers? Can you name them in French? As before, unless you are a horticulturist, this is truly a challenging puzzle.

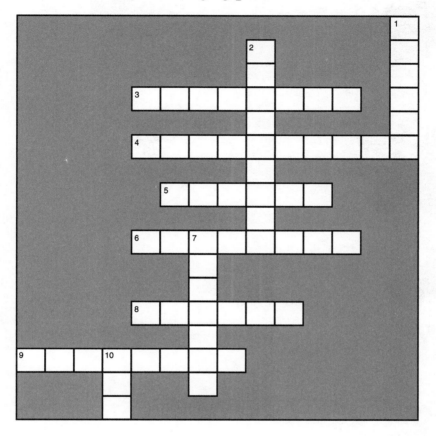

Across

3.

4.

Down

1.

2.

Across (continued)

Down (continued)

5.

7.

6.

10.

8.

9.

WORD CROSSES
Miscellaneous Grammar Topics

The word in the vertical column of each puzzle is related to the theme of the puzzle. This word is not given to you this time around, as it was previously. If you have forgotten your French grammar, simply consult the Grammar Charts section at the back.

81. The Present Indicative of Irregular Verbs
(Le présent de l'indicatif des verbes irréguliers)

As in the word crosses of the previous part, each clue consists of a French infinitive and a pronoun. The latter indicates the present indicative form you are required to figure out. If you know your irregular verbs, this puzzle will hardly pose a challenge to you.

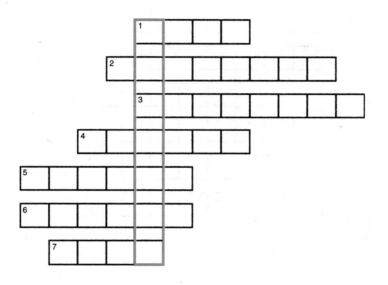

Clues

1. (pouvoir) il ...
2. (prendre) elles ...
3. (écrire) ils ...
4. (dire) elles ...
5. (être) nous ...
6. (boire) nous ...
7. (faire) elles ...

82. The Future and Conditional of Irregular Verbs
(Le futur et le conditionnel des verbes irréguliers)

As in the previous word cross puzzle, each clue consists of a French infinitive and a pronoun. The latter indicates the future or conditional form you are required to figure out. Again, if you know your irregular verbs, this puzzle will hardly pose a challenge to you, since most (but not all) are irregular.

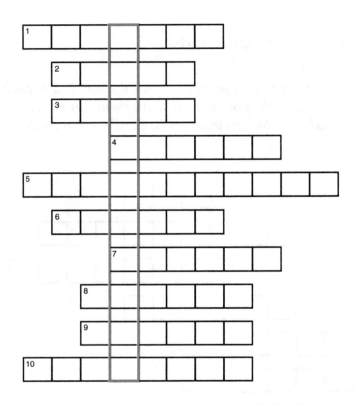

Clues

1. (avoir) nous …
2. (être) je …
3. (faire) vous …
4. (écrire) elle …
5. (manger) ils …
6. (savoir) tu …
7. (lire) elle …
8. (dire) nous …
9. (devoir) je …
10. (pouvoir) je …

83. Question Structures (Les structures interrogatives)

The clues are sentences from which the required question words are missing. This is certainly a challenging puzzle if you do not know how to ask questions! If you do not, this is your chance to learn.

Clues

1. ... joue au base-ball?
2. ... dis-tu?
3. ... est arrivé?
4. ... tu fais aujourd'hui?
5. Combien ... il veut?
6. Où ... tu vas?
7. ... allez-vous?
8. ... livre est-ce qu'il a?
9. ... m'as-tu menti?
10. ... seras-tu à Londres?
11. ... de personnes sont venues?

84. Noun Plurals Again (Les pluriels des noms encore une fois)

As in puzzle 31, the clues are the singular forms of the required plural nouns. This is a challenging puzzle only if you do not know your noun plurals!

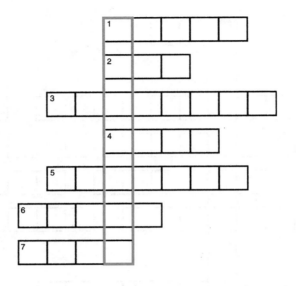

Clues

1. aïeul
2. nez
3. caillou
4. mois

5. travail
6. vieux
7. oeil

85. Adverbs (Les adverbes)

The clues are sentences from which the required adverbs are missing. This is certainly a challenging puzzle if you do not know your adverbs! This is your chance to learn.

Clues

1. Je ne reviendrai …
2. J'ai … fini mes devoirs.
3. Il va à Paris …
4. À partir de … j'étudierai les adverbes.
5. Ils s'aimeront …
6. Je ne me sens pas …
7. Passez … puisque vous êtes pressé.
8. L'avion passe … au-dessus de la maison.

SCRAMBLED LETTERS
Travel and Transportation
(Les voyages et le transport)

The first column contains the scrambled letters of the word or expression to which the clue in the middle column applies. Unscramble the letters, and write the answer in the third column.

86. Cars (Les autos)

Each clue either describes an automobile part or what the part allows one to do.

Scrambled Letters	Clues	Answers
1. VLANOT	il permet de "tourner" ou conduire l'auto	_____
2. EPNU	composant de l'auto "en caoutchouc"	_____
3. RECOFF	où se trouve le pneu de rechange	_____
4. POCAT	il couvre le moteur	_____
5. PREA-BSERI	vitre protecteur	_____
6. PREA-COCHS	il amortit les chocs	_____
7. PREHAS	les "lumières" de l'auto	_____
8. FEIRN	il permet d'arrêter l'auto	_____

87. Airports and Airplanes (Les aéroports et les avions)

The clues are descriptions or synonyms referring to flight personnel and air travel.

Scrambled Letters	Clues	Answers
1. CRTAE D'ERQUEMBAMENT	elle est nécessaire pour embarquer	_____
2. SWARTED	l'homme de service pendant le vol	_____
3. CMANDOMANT	le pilote	_____
4. SÈGIE	où s'assied un passager	_____
5. CTUREINE ED SRITÉCUÉ	elle est nécessaire pour la sécurité des passagers	_____
6. HTESSÔE (*f.*)	la femme de service pendant le vol	_____
7. DOLLAÉCGE (*m.*)	le contraire de "atterrissage"	_____

88. Trains and Buses (Les trains et les autobus)

The clues are descriptions or synonyms referring to train and bus travel.

Scrambled Letters	Clues	Answers
1. HRAIROE	il contient des informations relatives aux départs, etc.	_____
2. RGAE	il faut y aller pour prendre le train	_____
3. RGAE UROTIÈRE	il faut y aller pour prendre l'autobus	_____
4. LNEIG D'AOBUUTS	le "service" relatif à l'autobus	_____
5. CMINHE ED ERF	le "parcours" des trains	_____
6. BLLEIT	le "ticket" pour le train	_____

89. Hotels (Les hôtels)

The clues describe things associated with hotels.

Scrambled Letters	Clues	Answers
1. EPTIORÉCN (f.)	il faut y aller pour faire le "check in" à l'hôtel	_____
2. RERVAÉSTION (f.)	elle est nécessaire pour être sûr d'avoir une chambre à l'hôtel	_____
3. ARTCE ED CRDITÉ (f.)	elle est nécessaire pour les paiements	_____
4. CAMBHRE (f.)	où on dort dans l'hôtel	_____
5. PSCIINE (f.)	où on peut nager	_____

90. Vacations (Les vacances)

The clues are phrases from which are missing words referring to vacation spots (abroad, resort, etc.).

Scrambled Letters	Clues	Answers
1. À L'ÉNGETRAR	aller ... pour les vacances	_____
2. BNÉAIRALE	station ...	_____
3. EIVALSTE	station ... (= en été)	_____
4. HVEIR	station de sports d'...	_____
5. ONTAGMNE	à la ...	_____
6. EMR	en ...	_____

WORD SEARCHES

Computers and Technology
(Les ordinateurs et la technologie)

The hidden words can be found by reading in any of three directions: from left to right, from right to left, and top down. Circle them.

91. Computers (Les ordinateurs)

The clues are either synonyms or descriptions of computer components (screen, mouse, etc.).

V	B	T	Y	U	I	O	O	P	L	J	N	S
D	C	A	S	É	I	O	O	P	L	J	N	O
D	C	A	S	C	I	O	O	P	L	J	N	U
D	I	M	P	R	I	M	A	N	T	E	C	R
D	C	A	S	A	I	O	O	P	L	J	N	I
O	R	D	I	N	A	T	E	U	R	S	A	S
V	B	T	Y	U	I	O	O	P	L	J	N	E
V	B	T	Y	U	I	O	O	P	L	J	N	R
D	M	O	N	I	T	E	U	R	U	I	O	T

Clues
1. dispositif qui imprime sur feuilles
2. surface sur laquelle se reproduit une image
3. le "computer"
4. appareil connecté à l'ordinateur qui permet d'opérer des sélections
5. écran d'un ordinateur

92. Television (La télévisión)

The clues are descriptions of concepts and things (program, remote control, etc.) related to television.

U	U	S	C	D	A	S	E	R	T	Y	U	I	T
B	B	I	C	D	A	S	E	R	T	Y	U	I	É
U	U	T	C	D	A	S	E	R	T	Y	U	I	L
R	R	C	C	D	A	S	E	R	T	Y	U	I	É
P	R	O	G	R	A	M	M	E	C	V	B	N	V
N	B	M	C	D	A	S	E	R	T	Y	U	I	I
C	V	B	N	M	P	O	I	H	G	T	R	S	S
S	O	A	P	-	O	P	É	R	A	M	L	E	E
C	V	B	N	M	P	O	I	H	G	T	R	S	U
T	É	L	É	C	O	M	M	A	N	D	E	A	R

Clues

1. ce qui est annoncé
2. comédie populaire produite pour la télévision
3. feuilleton télévisé populaire
4. dispositif recepteur de télévision
5. dispositif permettant de régler le téléviseur

93. Internet (Internet)

The clues are either synonyms or descriptions of Internet concepts (e-mail, Web site, etc.).

```
C  A  D  S  S  U  R  F  E  R  C  A  D  S
C  A  D  S  I  B  N  M  L  O  P  Y  T  R
C  A  D  S  T  B  N  M  L  O  P  S  P  P
C  A  D  S  E  -  M  A  I  L  P  E  P  P
B  N  M  L  O  P  Y  T  R  C  V  R  V  V
B  N  M  L  O  P  Y  T  R  C  V  V  V  V
B  N  M  L  O  P  Y  T  R  C  V  E  V  V
A  N  A  V  I  G  U  E  R  S  C  U  A  D
B  N  M  L  O  P  Y  T  R  C  V  R  B  N
```

Clues

1. "lieu" proposé par un serveur
2. courrier électronique
3. l'ordinateur regroupant les informations à partager sur un réseau
4. passer de site en site
5. synonyme de "surfer"

94. Communications (Les communications)

The clues are either synonyms or descriptions of communications technology (cell phone, satellite dish, etc.).

```
C   A   D   S   M   L   D   C   V   B   N   M   O   I
P   O   R   T   A   B   L   E   V   B   N   M   O   I
C   A   D   S   M   L   D   L   V   B   N   M   O   I
A   P   A   R   A   B   O   L   I   Q   U   E   A   S
C   A   D   S   M   L   D   U   S   A   D   C   L   M
C   A   D   S   M   L   D   L   S   A   D   C   L   M
C   A   D   S   M   L   D   A   S   A   D   C   L   M
C   A   D   S   M   L   D   I   S   A   D   C   L   M
N   M   K   L   P   O   T   R   É   S   E   A   U   A
S   D   C   C   Â   B   L   E   B   N   M   O   P   P
```

Clues

1. téléphone portable
2. le "satellite dish" (antenne …)
3. télévision par fil conducteur
4. ensemble de voies de communication
5. ordinateur qu'on peut porter

95. The Phone (Le téléphone)

The clues are either synonyms or descriptions of phone concepts (subscriber, long-distance, etc.).

B	N	M	H	G	F	D	S	A	E	D	R	T	E
B	N	M	H	G	F	D	S	A	R	O	R	T	E
I	N	T	E	R	U	R	B	A	I	N	S	A	E
B	N	M	H	G	F	D	S	B	O	N	S	A	E
B	N	M	H	G	F	D	S	O	O	E	H	G	F
G	T	É	L	É	P	H	O	N	E	R	H	G	F
B	N	M	H	G	F	D	S	N	Z	P	H	G	F
H	G	F	D	G	T	É	L	É	C	A	R	T	E

Clues
1. qui a pris un abonnement
2. communication téléphonique entre villes
3. communiquer par téléphone
4. ... et recevoir un coup de téléphone
5. carte de téléphone

CRYPTOGRAMS
French Culture (La culture française)

A specific number will correspond to a specific letter in all the cryptograms. For example, if you establish that 1 = H in any one of the five puzzles, then you can go ahead and substitute H for each occurrence of the digit 1 in the remaining puzzles. These challenging puzzles test your knowledge of French culture.

96. Writers (Les écrivains)

1. l'auteur de: *Les fleurs du mal* (Charles ...)

$\overline{1}\ \overline{2}\ \overline{3}\ \overline{4}\ \overline{5}\ \overline{6}\ \overline{2}\ \overline{7}\ \overline{8}\ \overline{5}$

2. l'auteur de: *Le bourgeois gentilhomme* (Jean-Baptiste ...)

$\overline{9}\ \overline{10}\ \overline{6}\ \overline{7}\ \overline{5}\ \overline{8}\ \overline{5}$

97. Artists (Les artistes)

1. peintre impressionniste (1841–1919): Pierre Auguste ...

$\overline{8}\ \overline{5}\ \overline{11}\ \overline{10}\ \overline{7}\ \overline{8}$

2. sculpteur innovateur (1840–1917): François-Auguste ...

$\overline{8}\ \overline{10}\ \overline{4}\ \overline{7}\ \overline{11}$

98. Musicians (Les musiciens)

1. le compositeur de *Carmen*: Georges ...

$\overline{1}\ \overline{7}\ \overline{12}\ \overline{5}\ \overline{13}$

2. compositeur né en Pologne connu comme "le poète du piano": Frédéric-François ...

$\overline{14}\ \overline{15}\ \overline{10}\ \overline{16}\ \overline{7}\ \overline{11}$

99. Film Directors (Les réalisateurs du cinéma)

1. réalisateur du film *La Chienne* (1931): Jean …

$\overline{8}\ \overline{5}\ \overline{11}\ \overline{10}\ \overline{7}\ \overline{8}$

2. réalisateur du film *A bout de souffle (Breathless)* (1959): Jean-Luc …

$\overline{17}\ \overline{10}\ \overline{4}\ \overline{2}\ \overline{8}\ \overline{4}$

100. Mathematicians (Les mathématiciens)

1. l'inventeur de la "géométrie analytique": René …

$\overline{4}\ \overline{5}\ \overline{18}\ \overline{14}\ \overline{2}\ \overline{8}\ \overline{13}\ \overline{5}\ \overline{18}$

2. l'inventeur de la téorie de la probabilité: Blaise …

$\overline{16}\ \overline{2}\ \overline{18}\ \overline{14}\ \overline{2}\ \overline{6}$

Answers

1.

2.

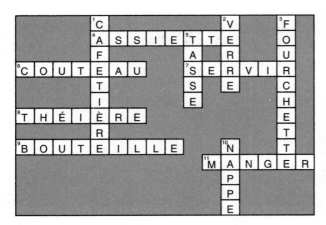

3.

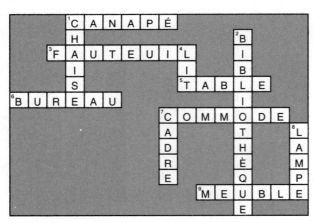

4.

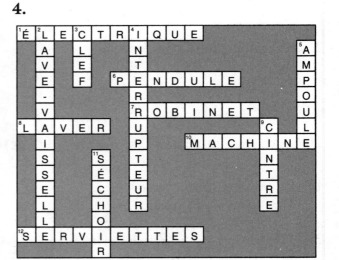

5.

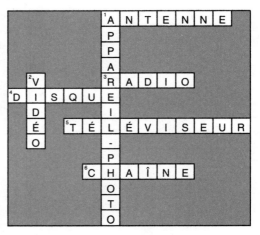

6.

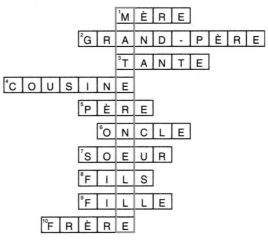

7.

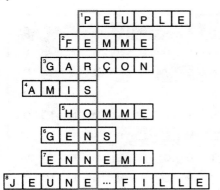

```
      ¹P E U P L E
      ²F E M M E
     ³G A R Ç O N
  ⁴A M I S
      ⁵H O M M E
   ⁶G E N S
    ⁷E N N E M I
⁸J E U N E … F I L L E
```

8.

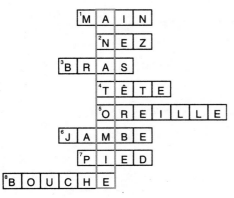

```
  ¹M A I N
    ²N E Z
 ³B R A S
    ⁴T Ê T E
     ⁵O R E I L L E
 ⁶J A M B E
   ⁷P I E D
⁸B O U C H E
```

9.

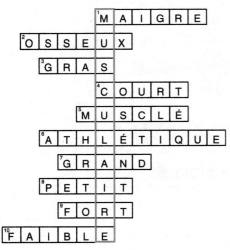

```
    ¹M A I G R E
²O S S E U X
  ³G R A S
      ⁴C O U R T
    ⁵M U S C L É
  ⁶A T H L É T I Q U E
    ⁷G R A N D
   ⁸P E T I T
   ⁹F O R T
¹⁰F A I B L E
```

10.

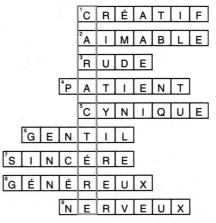

```
      ¹C R É A T I F
      ²A I M A B L E
      ³R U D E
   ⁴P A T I E N T
      ⁵C Y N I Q U E
 ⁶G E N T I L
⁷S I N C É R E
⁸G É N É R E U X
    ⁹N E R V E U X
```

11.
1. douze
2. soixante-dix
3. quatre-vingts
4. trois cents
5. un tiers
6. mille
7. un million
8. premier
9. quinzième
10. vingt-et-unième

12.
1. midi
2. minuit
3. une heure cinq
4. une heure et demie
5. deux heures et quart
6. dix heures du matin
7. dix heures du soir
8. deux heures de l'après-midi

13.
1. nuageux
2. couvert
3. soleil
4. vent
5. froid
6. chaud
7. pleut
8. neige

14.
1. rouge
2. bleu
3. vert
4. jaune
5. brun
6. violet
7. rose
8. blanc
9. noir
10. orange

15.
1. doux
2. amer
3. dur
4. mou
5. rond
6. lisse
7. ondulé
8. mouillé
9. sec

16.

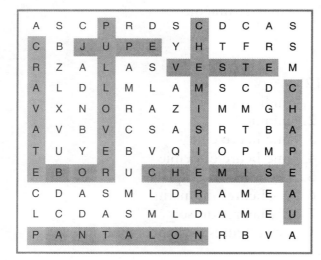

1. pantalon
2. chapeau
3. cravate
4. veste
5. chemise
6. chemisier
7. jupe
8. robe
9. pullover

17.

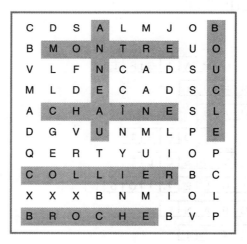

1. botte
2. chaussette
3. chaussure
4. bas
5. sandale
6. talon
7. semelle
8. lacet

18.

1. montre
2. anneau
3. collier
4. chaîne
5. boucle (d'oreille)
6. broche

19.

C	D	A	S	M	L	D	A	M	E	L	C
B	B	N	M	C	Z	C	X	S	A	Q	W
P	O	R	T	E	F	E	U	I	L	L	E
A	U	S	D	I	F	G	H	J	L	Z	C
V	T	N	Q	N	E	R	É	V	N	Z	O
V	O	B	N	T	Q	A	C	Z	C	D	E
E	N	A	S	U	M	L	H	C	D	A	S
X	X	X	Z	R	B	G	A	N	T	N	M
V	F	D	C	E	Z	A	R	S	O	D	P
C	D	A	S	M	L	E	P	C	L	M	A
S	A	B	O	U	R	S	E	B	N	M	A

1. bourse
2. gant
3. écharpe
4. ceinture
5. bouton
6. portefeuille

20.

A	S	C	D	L	M	H	L	A	M	E
C	V	B	M	C	H	A	N	G	E	R
C	V	E	B	U	I	B	L	M	N	C
D	É	S	H	A	B	I	L	L	E	R
A	A	S	A	A	B	L	A	S	C	D
C	C	A	C	C	I	L	A	S	C	D
C	C	Y	C	C	M	E	T	T	R	E
D	D	E	D	D	E	R	A	S	C	D
E	E	R	E	E	G	H	A	S	C	D

1. habiller (s'habiller)
2. mettre
3. changer (se changer)
4. déshabiller (se déshabiller)
5. essayer

21.
1. Bonjour!
2. Au revoir!

22.
1. Je m'appelle
2. Enchanté!

23.
1. nom
2. nom de famille

24.
1. rue
2. J'habite au …

25.
1. Allô!
2. numéro (de téléphone)

26.

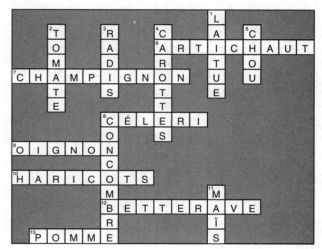

27.

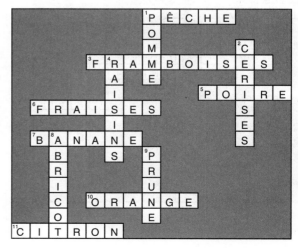

28.

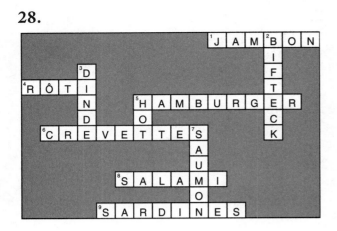

29.

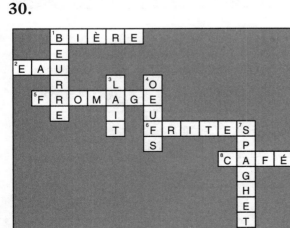

30.

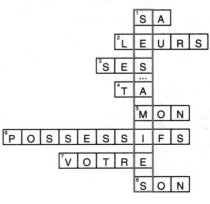

31.

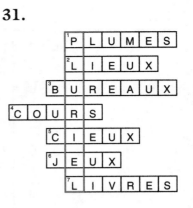

32.

33.

34.

35.

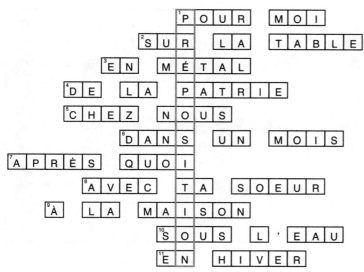

1. POUR MOI
2. SUR LA TABLE
3. EN MÉTAL
4. DE LA PATRIE
5. CHEZ NOUS
6. DANS UN MOIS
7. APRÈS QUOI
8. AVEC TA SOEUR
9. À LA MAISON
10. SOUS L'EAU
11. EN HIVER

36.
1. boire
2. eau
3. faim
4. soif
5. à la santé
6. vin
7. boisson non alcoolisée
8. limonade
9. orangeade

37.
1. menu
2. pourboire
3. garçon
4. serveuse
5. commande
6. portion
7. réservation

38.
1. manger
2. couper
3. sentir
4. verser
5. servir
6. prendre
7. renverser

39.
1. salé
2. épicé
3. doux
4. grillé
5. rôti
6. au four
7. mûr
8. aigre

40.
1. bien cuit
2. en sauce
3. salade de fruits
4. hors d'oeuvre
5. fruits de mer
6. purée de pommes de terre

41.

E	R	T	U	I	B	N	M	L	O	C	S	C
A	D	L	B	H	J	C	A	D	S	G	R	A
A	D	L	A	H	J	C	A	D	S	G	R	P
A	D	L	N	H	J	C	A	D	S	É	S	I
B	A	N	L	I	E	U	S	A	R	D	S	T
A	D	L	I	H	J	C	A	D	S	I	S	A
E	R	T	E	H	J	C	A	D	S	F	S	L
A	D	L	U	H	J	C	A	D	S	I	A	E
A	D	L	E	H	J	C	A	D	S	C	H	J
A	D	L	E	U	P	O	N	T	A	E	H	J
E	R	T	U	I	B	N	M	L	O	C	S	A
E	U	E	L	L	I	V	N	M	L	O	C	S

1. édifice
2. pont
3. capitale
4. banlieue
5. banlieusard
6. (centre-)ville

42.

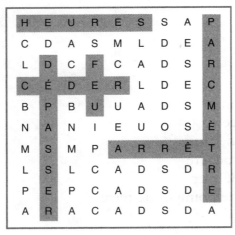

1. feu (de signalisation)
2. céder (le passage)
3. parcmètre
4. arrêt
5. dépasser
6. heures (de pointe)

43.

C	A	D	S	D	M	L	D	E	L	C	A	C		
C	A	D	S	D	M	L	D	E	L	C	A	R		
R	O	U	T	E	R	R	R	R	G	A	A	O		
B	P	H	R	R	F	F	F	F	R	S	S	I		
B	P	H	O	T	J	J	J	J	A	D	D	S		
S	O	U	T	E	R	R	A	I	N	M	M	E		
B	P	H	T	D	M	L	D	E	D	L	L	M		
M	L	D	O	T	J	J	J	J	E	E	E	E		
B	P	H	I	D	M	L	D	E	M	R	R	N		
M	L	D	R	T	J	J	J	J	L	G	G	T		
L	D	E	R	U	E	L	L	E	E	T	T	H		

1. route
2. ruelle
3. croisement
4. trottoir
5. (passage) souterrain
6. grande (route)

44.

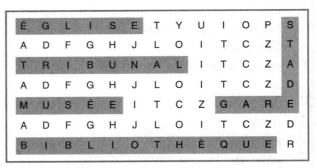

1. église
2. musée
3. bibliothèque
4. tribunal
5. stade
6. gare

45.

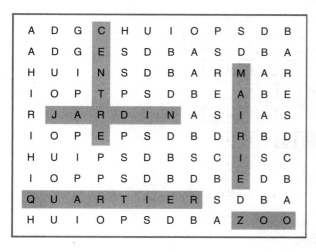

1. jardin
2. centre
3. quartier
4. mairie
5. zoo

46.
1. Merci!
2. Bienvenue!

47.
1. Excusez-moi!
2. S'il vous plaît!

48.
1. C'est impossible!
2. C'est faux que …

49.
1. Certainement!
2. Je ne suis pas d'accord!

50.
1. D'accord!
2. Peut-être!

51.

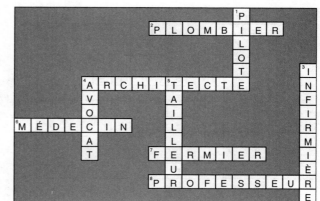

52.

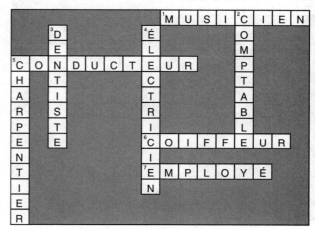

53.

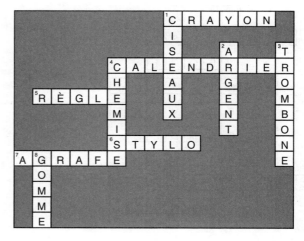

54.

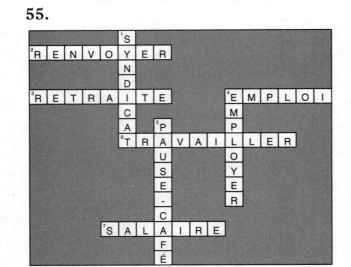

```
                              ¹F E R M E
²B U R E A U ³U              A
            N         ⁴C A B I N E T
            I         R
            V      ⁵S O C I É T É
            E         Q
            ⁶R E S T A U R A N T
            S         E
⁷M A G A S I N
            T
            ⁸É C O L E
```

55.

```
                ¹S
²R E N V O Y E R
                Y
                N
                D
³R E T R A I T E          ⁴E M P L O I
                C        M
                A   ⁵P    P
                ⁶T R A V A I L L E R
                    U    O
                    S    Y
                    E    E
                    -    R
                    C
            ⁷S A L A I R E
                    F
                    É
```

56.

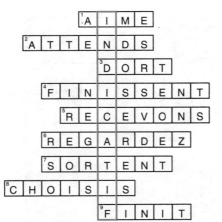

```
        ¹A I M E
    ²A T T E N D S
            ³D O R T
      ⁴F I N I S S E N T
        ⁵R E C E V O N S
      ⁶R E G A R D E Z
      ⁷S O R T E N T
  ⁸C H O I S I S
            ⁹F I N I T
```

57.

```
        ¹P U
        ²A I M É
³D O R M I
    ⁴É T É
    ⁵F I N I
⁶R O M P U
        ⁷E U
        ⁸S U
```

58.

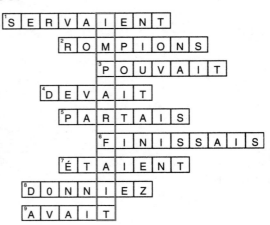

```
¹S E R V A I E N T
    ²R O M P I O N S
        ³P O U V A I T
  ⁴D E V A I T
  ⁵P A R T A I S
        ⁶F I N I S S A I S
    ⁷É T A I E N T
⁸D O N N I E Z
⁹A V A I T
```

59.

```
¹A I M E R A I
    ²R É U S S I R A
³C H A N G E R O N S
    ⁴R O U G I R A S
    ⁵C O L O R E R E Z
⁶D O R M I R A I
    ⁷R E C E V R O N T
⁸V E N D R A
```

60.

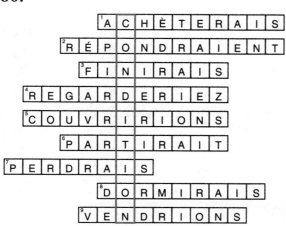

```
¹A C H È T E R A I S
²R É P O N D R A I E N T
  ³F I N I R A I S
⁴R E G A R D E R I E Z
⁵C O U V R I R I O N S
  ⁶P A R T I R A I T
⁷P E R D R A I S
    ⁸D O R M I R A I S
  ⁹V E N D R I O N S
```

61.
1. base-ball
2. football américain
3. basket
4. tennis
5. hockey
6. football
7. golf
8. gymnastique
9. ski

62.
1. patinoire
2. stade
3. court
4. terrain
5. gymnase
6. piste

63.
1. jeu de dames
2. échecs
3. jeu aux cartes
4. mots croisés
5. puzzle

64.
1. faire des courses
2. aller au cinéma
3. passe-temps
4. lecture
5. faire une promenade
6. aller nager

65.
1. faire du camping
2. vacances
3. prendre de l'exercice
4. jouer aux sports
5. faire du jogging

66.

```
A O R U R G E N C E H U A
S P A S D C M L G H J I M
R É A N I M A T I O N B B
A R A S D C M L G H J I U
M A T E R N I T É M L E L
C T A S D C M L G H J I A
A I A S D C M L G H J I N
D O O U S A L L E P H D C
S N A S D C M L G H J I E
```

1. salle
2. réanimation
3. opération
4. maternité
5. ambulance
6. urgence

67.

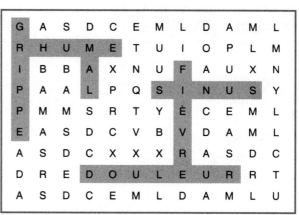

```
G A S D C E M L D A M L
R H U M E T U I O P L M
I B B A X N U F A U X N
P A A L P Q S I N U S Y
P M M S R T Y È C E M L
E A S D C V B V D A M L
A S D C X X X R A S D C
D R E D O U L E U R R T
A S D C E M L D A M L U
```

1. fièvre
2. douleur
3. mal (de tête)
4. sinus
5. rhume
6. grippe

68.

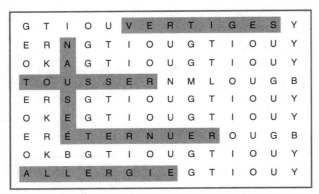

1. cavité
2. plombage
3. carie
4. (se) laver (les dents)
5. dentier

69.

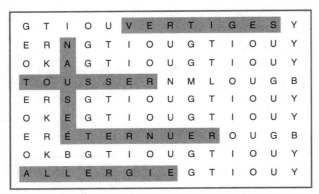

1. tousser
2. vertiges
3. nausée
4. allergie
5. éternuer

70.

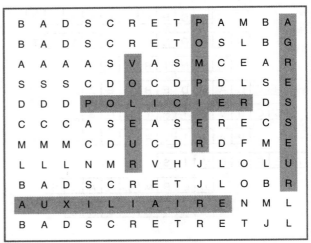

1. voleur
2. policier
3. pompier
4. auxiliare (médicale)
5. agresseur

71.
1. coupe de cheveux
2. permanente

72.
1. vernis à ongles
2. maquillage

73.
1. bonheur
2. tristesse

74.
1. imagination
2. bêtise

75.
1. égoïste
2. altruiste

76.

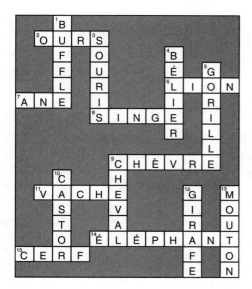

77.

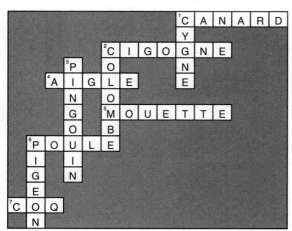

78.

79.

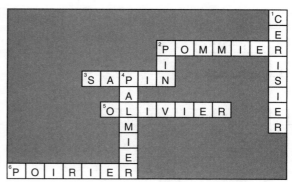

80.

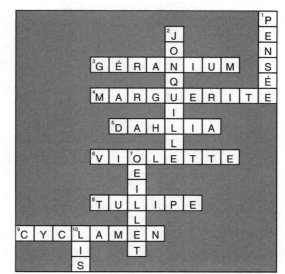

81.

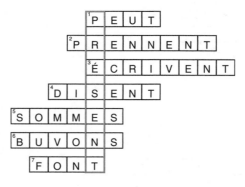

82.

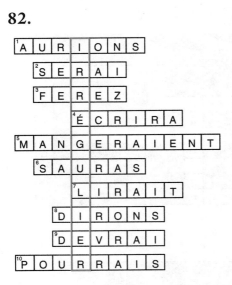

¹A	U	R	I	O	N	S

²S E R A I

³F E R E Z

⁴É C R I R A

⁵M A N G E R A I E N T

⁶S A U R A S

⁷L I R A I T

⁸D I R O N S

⁹D E V R A I

¹⁰P O U R R A I S

83.

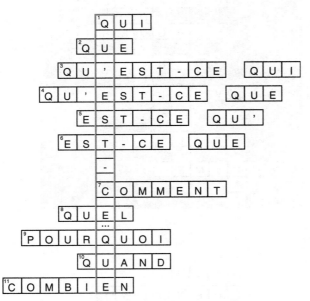

¹Q U I

²Q U E

³Q U ' E S T - C E   Q U I

⁴Q U ' E S T - C E   Q U E

⁵E S T - C E   Q U '

⁶E S T - C E   Q U E

-

⁷C O M M E N T

⁸Q U E L ...

⁹P O U R Q U O I

¹⁰Q U A N D

¹¹C O M B I E N

84.

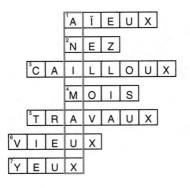

¹A Ï E U X

²N E Z

³C A I L L O U X

⁴M O I S

⁵T R A V A U X

⁶V I E U X

⁷Y E U X

85.

¹J A M A I S

²D É J A

³S O U V E N T

⁴M A I N T E N A N T

⁵T O U J O U R S

⁶B I E N

⁷D E V A N T

⁸J U S T E

86.
1. volant
2. pneu
3. coffre
4. capot
5. pare-brise
6. pare-chocs
7. phares
8. frein

87.
1. carte d'embarquement
2. steward
3. commandant
4. siège
5. ceinture de sécurité
6. hôtesse
7. décollage

88.
1. horaire
2. gare
3. gare routière
4. ligne d'autobus
5. chemin de fer
6. billet

89.
1. réception
2. réservation
3. carte de crédit
4. chambre
5. piscine

90.
1. à l'étranger
2. balnéaire
3. estivale
4. hiver
5. montagne
6. mer

91.

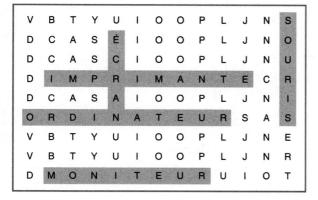

1. imprimante
2. écran
3. ordinateur
4. souris
5. moniteur

92.

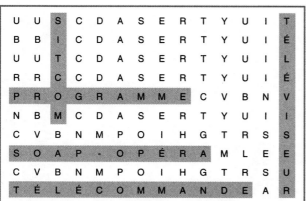

1. programme
2. sitcom
3. soap-opéra
4. téléviseur
5. télécommande

93.

C	A	D	S	S	U	R	F	E	R	C	A	D	S
C	A	D	S	I	B	N	M	L	O	P	Y	T	R
C	A	D	S	T	B	N	M	L	O	P	S	P	P
C	A	D	S	E	-	M	A	I	L	P	E	P	P
B	N	M	L	O	P	Y	T	R	C	V	R	V	V
B	N	M	L	O	P	Y	T	R	C	V	V	V	V
B	N	M	L	O	P	Y	T	R	C	V	E	V	V
A	N	A	V	I	G	U	E	R	S	C	U	A	D
B	N	M	L	O	P	Y	T	R	C	V	R	B	N

1. site
2. e-mail
3. serveur
4. surfer
5. naviguer

94.

C	A	D	S	M	L	D	C	V	B	N	M	O	I
P	O	R	T	A	B	L	E	V	B	N	M	O	I
C	A	D	S	M	L	D	L	V	B	N	M	O	I
A	P	A	R	A	B	O	L	I	Q	U	E	A	S
C	A	D	S	M	L	D	U	S	A	D	C	L	M
C	A	D	S	M	L	D	L	S	A	D	C	L	M
C	A	D	S	M	L	D	A	S	A	D	C	L	M
C	A	D	S	M	L	D	I	S	A	D	C	L	M
N	M	K	L	P	O	T	R	É	S	E	A	U	A
S	D	C	C	Â	B	L	E	B	N	M	O	P	P

1. cellulaire
2. parabolique
3. câble
4. réseau
5. portable

95.

B	N	M	H	G	F	D	S	A	E	D	R	T	E
B	N	M	H	G	F	D	S	A	R	O	R	T	E
I	N	T	E	R	U	R	B	A	I	N	S	A	E
B	N	M	H	G	F	D	S	B	O	N	S	A	E
B	N	M	H	G	F	D	S	O	O	E	H	G	F
G	T	É	L	É	P	H	O	N	E	R	H	G	F
B	N	M	H	G	F	D	S	N	Z	P	H	G	F
H	G	F	D	G	T	É	L	É	C	A	R	T	E

1. abonné
2. interurbain
3. téléphoner
4. donner
5. télécarte

96.
1. Baudelaire (Charles)
2. Molière (Jean-Baptiste)

97.
1. Renoir (Pierre Auguste)
2. Rodin (François-Auguste)

98.
1. Bizet (Georges)
2. Chopin (Frédéric-François)

99.
1. Renoir (Jean)
2. Godard (Jean-Luc)

100.
1. Descartes (René)
2. Pascal (Blaise)

Grammar Charts

Noun Plurals (Puzzles 31 and 84)

1. The plural of nouns is generally formed by adding s at the end of the noun (as in English); the plural of nouns ending in au and eu (and some in ou) is formed by adding x instead:

Singular		Plural	
(la) plume	feather	(les) plumes	feathers
(le) livre	book	(les) livres	books
(le) bureau	desk	(les) bureaux	desks
(le) chou	cabbage	(les) choux	cabbages
(le) jeu	game	(les) jeux	games
(le) lieu	place	(les) lieux	places

2. Nouns ending in s, x, and z do not change; the plural of nouns ending in al and ail is formed by changing these endings to aux:

Singular		Plural	
(le) cours	course	(les) cours	courses
(le) vieux	old man	(les) vieux	old men
(le) nez	nose	(les) nez	noses
(le) cheval	horse	(les) chevaux	horses
(l') animal	animal	(les) animaux	animals
(le) travail	work	(les) travaux	works

3. Note the plural of aïeul, ciel, and oeil:

Singular		Plural	
(l') aïeul	grandparent	(les) aïeux	grandparents
(le) ciel	sky	(les) cieux	skies
(l') oeil	eye	(les) yeux	eyes

Adjectives (Puzzle 32)

In French dictionaries adjectives are given in the masculine form. The feminine is formed generally by adding e to the masculine adjective. However, an f ending is changed to ve in the feminine, an x ending to se or sometimes to ce or sse (with some exceptions), and an er ending to ère. Finally, if the masculine adjective ends in el, eil, en, et, or on, the final consonant is doubled before the e is added on in the feminine:

Masculine		Feminine	
élégant	elegant	élégante	elegant
vif	lively	vive	lively
heureux	happy	heureuse	happy
doux	sweet	douce	sweet
faux	wrong	fausse	wrong
vieux	old	vieille	old
amer	bitter	amère	bitter
bon	good	bonne	good

Demonstrative Adjectives (Puzzle 33)

The English demonstratives this and that are generally translated as follows: (1) by ce before a masculine form beginning with a consonant or aspirated h; (2) by cet before a masculine form beginning with a vowel or mute h; and by (3) cette before any feminine form. The plural forms these and those are rendered by the singly French demonstrative ces:

Masculine Singular		Masculine Plural	
ce livre	this/that book	ces livres	these/those books
cet imperméable	this/that raincoat	ces imperméables	these/those raincoats

Feminine Singular		Feminine Plural	
cette chemise	this/that shirt	ces chemises	these/those shirts
cette fenêtre	this/that window	ces fenêtres	these/those windows

Possessive Adjectives (Puzzle 34)

(fam. = familiar form, pol. = polite form, pl. = plural form, c. = before a consonant, v. = before a vowel)

Masculine Singular		Masculine Plural	
mon livre	my book	mes livres	my books
ton frère (fam.)	your brother	tes frères	your brothers
votre frère (pol.)	your brother	votres frères	your brothers
son oncle	his/her uncle	ses oncles	his aunt
notre livre	our book	nos livres	our books
votre cousin (pl.)	your cousin	vos cousins	your cousins
leur ami	their friend	leurs amis	their friends

Feminine Singular		Feminine Plural	
ma soeur (c.)	my sister	mes soeurs	my sisters
mon amie (v.)	my friend	mes amies	my friends
ta tante (c., fam.)	your aunt	tes tantes	your aunts
ton amie (v., fam.)	your friend	tes amies	your friends
votre tante (pol.)	your aunt	vos tantes	your aunts
sa soeur (c.)	his/her sister	ses soeurs	his/her sisters
son amie (v.)	his/her friend	ses amies	his/her friends
notre tante	our aunt	nos tantes	our aunts
votre cousine	your cousin	vos cousines	your cousins
leur amie	their friend	leurs amies	their friends

Prepositions (Puzzle 35)

French	English
à	at
après	after
avec	with
chez	with
dans	in
de	of
en	in
pour	for
sous	under
sur	on

Question Structures (Puzzle 83)

French	English
qui (Qui est venu?)	who, whom (Who came?)
que (Que dis-tu?)	what (What are you saying?)
quoi (De quoi est-ce qu'il parle?)	what (What is he talking about?)
qu'est-ce qui (Qu'est-ce qui est arrivé?)	what (What happened?)
qu'est-ce que (Qu'est-ce que vous faites?)	what (What are you doing?)
pourquoi	why
quand	when
comment	how
combien	how much, how many
où	where

Sample Conjugations of Regular Verbs (Puzzles 56, 57, 58, 59, 60)

aimer / to love

Singular	Plural	Singular	Plural
Present Indicative		**Past Indefinite**	
j'aime (I love)	nous aimons (we love)	j'ai aimé (I loved)	nous avons aimé (we loved)
tu aimes (you love)	vous aimez (you love)	tu as aimé (you loved)	vous avez aimé (you loved)
il/elle aime (he/she loves)	ils/elles aiment (they love)	il/elle a aimé (he/she loved)	ils/elles ont aimé (they loved)
Imperfect Indicative		**Future**	
j'aimais (I was loving)	nous aimions (we were loving)	j'aimerai (I will love)	nous aimerons (we will love)
tu aimais (you were loving)	vous aimiez (you were loving)	tu aimeras (you will love)	vous aimerez (you will love)
il/elle aimait (he/she was loving)	ils/elles aimaient (they were loving)	il/elle aimera (he/she will love)	ils/elles aimeront (they will love)
Conditional			
j'aimerais (I would love)		nous aimerions (we would love)	
tu aimerais (you would love)		vous aimeriez (you would love)	
il/elle aimerait (he/she would love)		ils/elles aimeraient (they would love)	

dormir / to sleep

Singular	Plural	Singular	Plural
Present Indicative		***Past Indefinite***	
je dors (I sleep)	nous dormons (we sleep)	j'ai dormi (I slept)	nous avons dormi (we slept)
tu dors (you sleep)	vous dormez (you sleep)	tu as dormi (you slept)	vous avez dormi (you slept)
il/elle dort (he/she sleeps)	ils/elles dorment (they sleep)	il/elle a dormi (he/she slept)	ils/elles ont dormi (they slept)
Imperfect Indicative		***Future***	
je dormais (I was sleeping)	nous dormions (we were sleeping)	je dormirai (I will sleep)	nous dormirons (we will sleep)
tu dormais (you were sleeping)	vous dormiez (you were sleeping)	tu dormiras (you will sleep)	vous dormirez (you will sleep)
il/elle dormait (he/she was sleeping)	ils/elles dormaient (they were sleeping)	il/elle dormira (he/she will sleep)	ils/elles dormiront (they will sleep)
Conditional			
je dormirais (I would sleep)		nous dormirions (we would sleep)	
tu dormirais (you would sleep)		vous dormiriez (you would sleep)	
il/elle dormirait (he/she would sleep)		ils/elles dormiraient (they would sleep)	

finir / to finish

Singular	Plural	Singular	Plural
Present Indicative		***Past Indefinite***	
je finis (I finish)	nous finissons (we finish)	j'ai fini (I finished)	nous avons fini (we finished)
tu finis (you finish)	vous finissez (you finish)	tu as fini (you finished)	vous avez fini (you finished)
il/elle finit (he/she finishes)	ils/elles finissent (they finish)	il/elle a fini (he/she finished)	ils/elles ont fini (they finished)
Imperfect Indicative		***Future***	
je finissais (I was finishing)	nous finissions (we were finishing)	je finirai (I will finish)	nous finirons (we will finish)
tu finissais (you were finishing)	vous finissiez (you were finishing)	tu finiras (you will finish)	vous finirez (you will finish)
il/elle finissait (he/she was finishing)	ils/elles finissaient (they were finishing)	il/elle finira (he/she will finish)	ils/elles finiront (they will finish)

Conditional

je finirais (I would finish)	nous finirions (we would finish)
tu finirais (you would finish)	vous finiriez (you would finish)
il/elle finirait (he/she would finish)	ils/elles finiraient (they would finish)

rompre / to break

Singular	Plural	Singular	Plural
Present Indicative		**Past Indefinite**	
je romps (I break)	nous rompons (we break)	j'ai rompu (I broke)	nous avons rompu (we broke)
tu romps (you break)	vous rompez (you break)	tu as rompu (you broke)	vous avez rompu (you broke)
il/elle rompt (he/she breaks)	ils/elles rompent (they break)	il/elle a rompu (he/she broke)	ils/elles ont rompu (they broke)
Imperfect Indicative		**Future**	
je rompais (I was breaking)	nous rompions (we were breaking)	je romprai (I will break)	nous romprons (we will break)
tu rompais (you were breaking)	vous rompiez (you were breaking)	tu rompras (you will break)	vous romprez (you will break)
il/elle rompait (he/she was breaking)	ils/elles rompaient (they were breaking)	il/elle rompra (he/she will break)	ils/elles rompront (they will break)

Conditional

je romprais (I would break)	nous romprions (we would break)
tu romprais (you would break)	vous rompriez (you would break)
il/elle romprait (he/she would break)	ils/elles rompraient (they would break)

Note: Some verbs are conjugated with être in the present perfect. One example will suffice:

aller / to go

Singular		Plural	
je suis allé/allée	I have gone	nous sommes allés/ allées	we have gone
tu es allé/allée	you have gone	vous êtes allés/allées	you have gone
il/elle est allé/allée	he/she has gone	ils/elles sont allés/ allées	they have gone

Irregular Verbs (Puzzles 57, 58, 81, 82)

avoir / to have

Present Indicative
(j')ai, (tu) as, (il/elle) a, (nous) avons, (vous) avez, (ils/elles) ont

Past Indefinite
(j')ai eu, (tu) as eu, (il/elle) a eu, (nous) avons eu, (vous) avez eu, (ils/elles) ont eu

Imperfect Indicative
(j')avais, (tu) avais, (il/elle) avait, (nous) avions, (vous) aviez, (ils/elles) avaient

Future
(j')aurai, (tu) auras, (il/elle) aura, (nous) aurons, (vous) aurez, (ils/elles) auront

Conditional
(j')aurais, (tu) aurais, (il/elle) aurait, (nous) aurions, (vous) auriez, (ils/elles) auraient

boire / to drink

Present Indicative
(je) bois, (tu) bois, (il/elle) boit, (nous) buvons, (vous) buvez, (ils/elles) boivent

Past Indefinite
(j')ai bu, (tu) as bu, (il/elle) a bu, (nous) avons bu, (vous) avez bu, (ils/elles) ont bu

Imperfect Indicative
(je) buvais, (tu) buvais, (il/elle) buvait, (nous) buvions, (vous) buviez, (ils/elles) buvaient

Future
(je) boirai, (tu) boiras, (il/elle) boira, (nous) boirons, (vous) boirez, (ils/elles) boiront

Conditional
(je) boirais, (tu) boirais, (il/elle) boirait, (nous) boirions, (vous) boiriez, (ils/elles) boiraient

devoir / to have to

Present Indicative
(je) dois, (tu) dois, (il/elle) doit, (nous) devons, (vous) devez, (ils/elles) doivent

Past Indefinite
(j')ai dû, (tu) as dû, (il/elle) a dû, (nous) avons dû, (vous) avez dû, (ils/elles) ont dû

Imperfect Indicative
(je) devais, (tu) devais, (il/elle) devait, (nous) devions, (vous) deviez, (ils/elles) devaient

Future
(je) devrai, (tu) devras, (il/elle) devra, (nous) devrons, (vous) devrez, (ils/elles) devront

Conditional
(je) devrais, (tu) devrais, (il/elle) devrait, (nous) devrions, (vous) devriez, (ils/elles) devraient

dire / to say

Present Indicative
(je) dis, (tu) dis, (il/elle) dit, (nous) disons, (vous) dîtes, (ils/elles) disent

Past Indefinite
(j')ai dit, (tu) as dit, (il/elle) a dit, (nous) avons dit, (vous) avez dit, (ils/elles) ont dit

Imperfect Indicative
(je) disais, (tu) disais, (il/elle) disait, (nous) disions, (vous) disiez, (ils/elles) disaient

Future
(je) dirai, (tu) diras, (il/elle) dira, (nous) dirons, (vous) direz, (ils/elles) diront

Conditional
(je) dirais, (tu) dirais, (il/elle) dirait, (nous) dirions, (vous) diriez, (ils/elles) diraient

écrire / to write

Present Indicative
(j')écris, (tu) écris, (il/elle) écrit, (nous) écrivons, (vous) écrivez, (ils/elles) écrivent

Past Indefinite
(j')ai écrit, (tu) as écrit, (il/elle) a écrit, (nous) avons écrit, (vous) avez écrit, (ils/elles) ont écrit

Imperfect Indicative
(j')écrivais, (tu) écrivais, (il/elle) écrivait, (nous) écrivions, (vous) écriviez, (ils/elles) écrivaient

Future
(j')écrirai, (tu) écriras, (il/elle) écrira, (nous) écrirons, (vous) écrirez, (ils/elles) écriront

Conditional
(j')écrirais, (tu) écrirais, (il/elle) écrirait, (nous) écririons, (vous) écririez, (ils/elles) écriraient

être / to be

Present Indicative
(je) suis, (tu) es, (il/elle) est, (nous) sommes, (vous) êtes, (ils/elles) sont

Past Indefinite
(j')ai été, (tu) as été, (il/elle) a été, (nous) avons été, (vous) avez été, (ils/elles) ont été

Imperfect Indicative
(j')étais, (tu) étais, (il/elle) était, (nous) étions, (vous) étiez, (ils/elles) étaient

Future
(je) serai, (tu) seras, (il/elle) sera, (nous) serons, (vous) serez, (ils/elles) seront

Conditional
(je) serais, (tu) serais, (il/elle) serait, (nous) serions, (vous) seriez, (ils/elles) seraient

faire / to do, to make

Present Indicative
(je) fais, (tu) fais, (il/elle) fait, (nous) faisons, (vous) faites, (ils/elles) font

Past Indefinite
(j')ai fait, (tu) as fait, (il/elle) a fait, (nous) avons fait, (vous) avez fait, (ils/elles) ont fait

Imperfect Indicative
(je) faisais, (tu) faisais, (il/elle) faisait, (nous) faisions, (vous) faisiez, (ils/elles) faisaient

Future
(je) ferai, (tu) feras, (il/elle) fera, (nous) ferons, (vous) ferez, (ils/elles) feront

Conditional
(je) ferais, (tu) ferais, (il/elle) ferait, (nous) ferions, (vous) feriez, (ils/elles) feraient

lire / to read

Present Indicative
(je) lis, (tu) lis, (il/elle) lit, (nous) lisons, (vous) lisez, (ils/elles) lisent

Past Indefinite
(j')ai lu, (tu) as lu, (il/elle) a lu, (nous) avons lu, (vous) avez lu, (ils/elles) ont lu

Imperfect Indicative
(je) lisais, (tu) lisais, (il/elle) lisait, (nous) lisions, (vous) lisiez, (ils/elles) lisaient

Future
(je) lirai, (tu) liras, (il/elle) lira, (nous) lirons, (vous) lirez, (ils/elles) liront

Conditional
(je) lirais, (tu) lirais, (il/elle) lirait, (nous) lirions, (vous) liriez, (ils/elles) liraient

manger / to eat

Present Indicative
(je) mange, (tu) manges, (il/elle) mange, (nous) mangeons, (vous) mangez, (ils/elles) mangent

Past Indefinite
(j')ai mangé, (tu) as mangé, (il/elle) a mangé, (nous) avons mangé, (vous) avez mangé, (ils/elles) ont mangé

Imperfect Indicative
(je) mangeais, (tu) mangeais, (il/elle) mangeait, (nous) mangeions, (vous) mangeiez, (ils/elles) mangeaient

Future
(je) mangerai, (tu) mangeras, (il/elle) mangera, (nous) mangerons, (vous) mangerez, (ils/elles) mangeront

Conditional
(je) mangerais, (tu) mangerais, (il/elle) mangerait, (nous) mangerions, (vous) mangeriez, (ils/elles) mangeraient

pouvoir / to be able to (can)

Present Indicative
(je) peux, (tu) peux, (il/elle) peut, (nous) pouvons, (vous) pouvez, (ils/elles) peuvent

Past Indefinite
(j')ai pu, (tu) as pu, (il/elle) a pu, (nous) avons pu, (vous) avez pu, (ils/elles) ont pu

Imperfect Indicative
(je) pouvais, (tu) pouvais, (il/elle) pouvait, (nous) pouvions, (vous) pouviez, (ils/elles) pouvaient

Future
(je) pourrai, (tu) pourras, (il/elle) pourra, (nous) pourrons, (vous) pourrez, (ils/elles) pourront

Conditional
(je) pourrais, (tu) pourrais, (il/elle) pourrait, (nous) pourrions, (vous) pourriez, (ils/elles) pourraient

prendre / to take

Present Indicative
(je) prends, (tu) prends, (il/elle) prend, (nous) prenons, (vous) prenez, (ils/elles) prennent

Past Indefinite
(j')ai pris, (tu) as pris, (il/elle) a pris, (nous) avons pris, (vous) avez pris, (ils/elles) ont pris

Imperfect Indicative
(je) prenais, (tu) prenais, (il/elle) prenait, (nous) prenions, (vous) preniez, (ils/elles) prenaient

Future
(je) prendrai, (tu) prendras, (il/elle) prendra, (nous) prendrons, (vous) prendrez, (ils/elles) prendront

Conditional
(je) prendrais, (tu) prendrais, (il/elle) prendrait, (nous) prendrions, (vous) prendriez, (ils/elles) prendraient

savoir / to know

Present Indicative
(je) sais, (tu) sais, (il/elle) sait, (nous) savons, (vous) savez, (ils/elles) savent

Past Indefinite
(j')ai su, (tu) as su, (il/elle) a su, (nous) avons su, (vous) avez su, (ils/elles) ont su

Imperfect Indicative
(je) savais, (tu) savais, (il/elle) savait, (nous) savions, (vous) saviez, (ils/elles) savaient

Future
(je) saurai, (tu) sauras, (il/elle) saura, (nous) saurons, (vous) saurez, (ils/elles) sauront

Conditional
(je) saurais, (tu) saurais, (il/elle) saurait, (nous) saurions, (vous) sauriez, (ils/elles) sauraient

Word Finder

The words and expressions below are the ones needed to solve the puzzles. They are listed here for your convenience.

m. = masculine
f. = feminine
pl. = plural

A

abonné *m.*	subscriber
abricot *m.*	apricot
acheterais (j')	I would buy
agrafe *f.*	staple
agresseur *m.*	assailant
aïeux *m. pl.*	grandparents
aigle *m.*	eagle
aigre	sour
aimable	kind
aimé	loved
aime (j')	I love
aimerai (j')	I will love
à la maison	at home
À votre santé!	To your health!
à l'étranger	abroad
aller au cinéma	to go to the movies
allergie *f.*	allergy
aller nager	to go for a swim
Allô!	Hello (on the phone)!
altruiste	altruistic
ambulance *f.*	ambulance
amer	bitter
amère *f.*	bitter
amis *m. pl.*	friends
ampoule *f.*	lightbulb
anatomique	anatomical
ancienne *f.*	ancient, old
âne *m.*	donkey

animaux *m. pl.*	animals
anneau *m.*	ring
antenne parabolique *f.*	satellite dish
appareil-photo *m.*	camera
après quoi	after which
arbre *m.*	tree
architecte *m.*	architect
argent *m.*	money
arrêt *m.*	stop
artichaut *m.*	artichoke
assiette *f.*	plate
athlétique	athletic
attends (tu)	you wait for
au four	baked
Au revoir!	Good-bye!
aurions (nous)	we would have
auxiliare médical *m.*	paramedic
avait (il)	he was having
avec ta soeur	with your sister
avocat *m.*	lawyer

B

balnéaire (station balnéaire)	seaside resort
banane *f.*	banana
banlieue *m.*	suburbs
banlieusard *m.*	suburbanite
bas *m.*	stocking
base-ball *m.*	baseball
basket *m.*	basketball
Baudelaire (Charles)	Baudelaire (Charles)
beignet *m.*	doughnut
bélier *m.*	ram
bêtise *f.*	foolishness
betterave *f.*	beet
beurre *m.*	butter
bibliothèque *f.*	bookcase

bien	well
bien cuit	well done
Bienvenue! *f.*	Welcome!
bière *f.*	beer
bifteck *m.*	steak
billet *m.*	train ticket
biscuits *m. pl.*	cookies, biscuits
Bizet (Georges)	Bizet (Georges)
blanc	white
bleu	blue
boire	to drink
boisson non alcoolisée *f.*	soft drink
bonheur *m.*	happiness
Bonjour!	Hello!
bonne *f.*	good
botte *f.*	boot
bouche *f.*	mouth
boucle (d'oreille) *f.*	earring
bourse *f.*	purse
bouteille *f.*	bottle
bouton *m.*	button
branche *f.*	branch
bras *m.*	arm
broche *f.*	brooch
brun	brown
buffle *m.*	buffalo
bureau *m.*	desk, office
bureaux *m. pl.*	desks
buvons (nous)	we drink

C

cabinet *m.*	doctor's office
câble *m.*	cable
cadre *m.*	frame
café *m.*	coffee
cafetière *f.*	coffeepot
cailloux *m. pl.*	stones
calendrier *m.*	calendar
canapé *m.*	couch, sofa
canard *m.*	duck
capitale *f.*	capital
capot *m.*	hood
caractère *m.*	character

carie *f.*	tooth decay
carottes *f. pl.*	carrots
carte de crédit *f.*	credit card
carte d'embarquement *f.*	boarding pass
castor *m.*	beaver
cavité *f.*	cavity
ce *m.*	this/that
céder le passage	yield
ceinture *f.*	belt
ceinture de sécurité *f.*	seatbelt
céleri *m.*	celery
cellulaire *m.*	cellphone
centre commercial *m.*	shopping mall
centre-ville *m.*	downtown, city center
cerf *m.*	deer
cerises *f. pl.*	cherries
cerisier *m.*	cherry tree
Certainment!	Certainly!
ces *pl.*	these/those
C'est faux que …	It's not true that …
C'est impossible!	It's impossible!
cet *m.*	this/that
cette *f.*	this/that
chaîne *f.*	chain
chaîne stéréo *f.*	stereo
chaise *f.*	chair
chambre *f.*	hotel room
chambre (à coucher) *f.*	bedroom
champignon *m.*	mushroom
changer (se changer)	to change
changerons (nous)	we will change
chapeau *m.*	hat
charpentier *m.*	carpenter
chaud	hot
chaussette *f.*	sock
chaussure *f.*	shoe
chemin de fer *m.*	railroad
chemise *f.*	shirt, file folder
chemisier *m.*	blouse

cheval *m.*	horse
chèvre *f.*	goat
chez nous	with us
choisis (je)	I choose
Chopin (Frédéric-François)	Chopin (Frédéric-François)
chou *m.*	cabbage
cieux *m. pl.*	skies
cigogne *f.*	stork
cintre *m.*	clothes hanger
ciseaux *m. pl.*	scissors
citron *m.*	lemon
clef *f.*	key
coffre *m.*	trunk
coiffeur *m.*	barber
collier *m.*	necklace
colombe *f.*	dove
colorez (vous)	you will color
combien	how many
commandant *m.*	flight captain
commande *f.*	order
comment	how
commode *f.*	dresser, chest of drawers
comptable *m.*	accountant
concombre *m.*	cucumber
condition *f.*	condition
conducteur *m.*	driver
confiture *f.*	jam
coq *m.*	rooster
coupe de cheveux *f.*	haircut
couper	to cut
cours *m. pl.*	courses
court	short
court *m.*	tennis court
cousine *f.*	cousin (female)
couteau *m.*	knife
couvert	overcast
couvrions (nous)	we would cover
cravate *f.*	tie
crayon *m.*	pencil
créatif	creative
crevettes *f. pl.*	shrimps
croisement *m.*	intersection
croissant *m.*	croissant
cuillère *f.*	spoon
cuisine *f.*	kitchen
cyclamen *m.*	cyclamen
cygne *m.*	swan
cynique	cynical

D

D'accord!	OK!
dahlia *m.*	dahlia
dans un mois	in a month
décollage *m.*	takeoff
déjà	already
de la patrie	of the country
dent *m.*	tooth
dentier *m.*	false teeth, dentures
dentiste *m.*	dentist
dépasser	to pass
Descartes (René)	Descartes (René)
déshabiller (se déshabiller)	to get undressed
deux heures de l'après-midi	two in the afternoon
deux heures et quart	a quarter past two
devait (elle)	she had to
devant	in front
devrai (je)	I will have to
dinde *f.*	turkey
dirons (nous)	we will say
disent (elles)	they say
disque compact *m.*	compact disc
dix heures du matin	ten in the morning
dix heures du soir	ten in the evening
donner un coup de téléphone	to make a call
donniez (vous)	you were giving
dormi	slept
dormirai (je)	I will sleep
dormirais (je)	I would sleep
dort (elle)	she sleeps
douce *f.*	sweet
doux	sweet
douze	twelve
dur	hard

E

eau *f.*	water
eau minérale *f.*	mineral water
écharpe *f.*	scarf
échecs *m. pl.*	chess
école *f.*	school
écran *m.*	screen
écrira (elle)	she will write
écrivent (ils)	they write
edifice *m.*	building
église *f.*	church
égöiste	egoistic
électricien *m.*	electrician
élégante *f.*	elegant
éléphant *m.*	elephant
e-mail *m.*	e-mail
emploi *m.*	employment
employé *m.*	office clerk
employer	to hire
en hiver	in winter
en métal	in metal
en sauce	in a sauce
Enchanté! *m.*	Pleased to meet you!
ennemi *m.*	enemy
entrée *f.*	entrance
épicé	spicy
escalier *m.*	stairs
essayer	to try on
estivale (station estivale)	summer resort
étaient (elles)	they were
été	has been
éternuer	to sneeze
eu	had
Excusez-moi!	Excuse me!

F

fabrique *f.*	factory
faible	weak
faim *f.*	hunger
faire du camping	to go camping
faire du jogging	to jog
faire les courses	to shop
faire une promenade	to go for a walk

fauteuil *m.*	armchair
femme *f.*	woman
fenêtre *f.*	window
ferez (vous)	you will make
ferme *f.*	farm
fermier *m.*	farmer
feu de signalisation *m.*	traffic light
feuille *f.*	leaf
fille *f.*	daughter
fils *m.*	son
fini	finished
finirais (tu)	you would finish
finissais (tu)	you were finishing
finissent (ils)	they finish
finit (il)	he finishes
fleur *f.*	flower
font (elles)	they make
football *m.*	soccer
football américain *m.*	football
fort	strong
fourchette *f.*	fork
fraises *f. pl.*	strawberries
framboises *f. pl.*	raspberries
frein *m.*	brake
frère *m.*	brother
frites *f. pl.*	fries
froid	cold
fromage *m.*	cheese
fruits de mer *m. pl.*	seafood

G

gant *m.*	glove
garage *m.*	garage
garçon *m.*	boy, waiter
gare *f.*	train station
gare routière *f.*	bus station
gâteau *m.*	cake
généreux	generous
gens *m. pl.*	people
gentil	nice
géranium *m.*	geranium
girafe *f.*	giraffe
glace *f.*	ice cream

Godard (Jean-Luc)	Godard (Jean-Luc)	jardin public *m.*	park
golf *m.*	golf	jaune	yellow
gomme *f.*	eraser	Je m'appelle …	My name is …
gorille *m.*	gorilla	Je ne suis pas d'accord!	I disagree!
graine *f.*	seed		
grand	tall, big	jeu au cartes *m.*	playing cards
grande route *f.*	highway	jeu de dames *m.*	checkers
grand-père *m.*	grandfather	jeune fille *f.*	girl
gras	fat	jeux *m. pl.*	games
grenier *m.*	attic	J'habite au …	I live at …
grillé	grilled	jonquille *f.*	daffodil
gymnase *m.*	gymnasium	jouer au sports	to play sports
gymnastique *f.*	gymnastics	jupe *f.*	skirt
		juste	just

H

habiller (s'habiller)	to get dressed
hamburger *m.*	hamburger
haricots *m. pl.*	beans
heures de pointe *f. pl.*	rush hour
hiver (station de sports d'hiver)	winter sports resort
hockey *m.*	hockey
homme *m.*	man
horaire *m.*	timetable, schedule
hors d'oeuvre *m.*	appetizer, starter
hot dog *m.*	hot dog
hôtesse *f.*	female flight attendant

I

imagination *f.*	imagination
imparfait	imperfect
imprimante *f.*	printer
indicatif	indicative
infirmière *f.*	nurse
interrupteur *m.*	switch
interurbain *m.*	long-distance call
irrégulier	irregular

J

jamais	never
jambe *f.*	leg
jambon *m.*	ham

L

lacet *m.*	lace
lait *m.*	milk
laitue *f.*	lettuce
lampe *f.*	lamp
lampe électrique *f.*	flashlight
laver (se laver les dents)	to brush one's teeth
lave-vaisselle *m.*	dishwasher
lecture *f.*	reading
leurs *m. pl.*	their
lieux *m. pl.*	places
ligne d'autobus *f.*	bus service
limonade *f.*	lemonade (fizzy)
lion *m.*	lion
lirait (elle)	she would read
lis *m.*	lily
lisse	smooth
lit *m.*	bed
livres *m. pl.*	books

M

machine à coudre *f.*	sewing machine
machine à laver *f.*	washer
magasin *m.*	store
maigre	thin, skinny
main *f.*	hand
maintenant	now
mairie *f.*	city hall

maïs *m.*	corn	nez *m.*	nose, noses
manger	to eat	noir	black
mangeraient (ils)	they would eat	nom *m.*	given (first) name
maquillage *m.*	makeup	nom de famille *m.*	surname (family name)
marguerite *f.*	daisy		
maternelle *f.*	maternal	numéro (téléphonique)	phone number
maternité *f.*	maternity		
mauvaise herbe *f.*	weed		
médecin *m.*	doctor	**O**	
menu *m.*	menu	oeillet *m.*	carnation
mer (en mer)	by the sea, at sea	oeufs *m. pl.*	eggs
Merci!	Thank you!	oignon *m.*	onion
mère *f.*	mother	olivier *m.*	olive tree
mettre	to put on	oncle *m.*	uncle
meuble *m.*	cabinet	ondulé	wavy
midi	noon	opération *f.*	operation
mille	one thousand	orange (noun *f.* and adj.)	orange
million (un million)	one million		
minuit	midnight	orangeade *f.*	orangeade
mois *m. pl.*	months	ordinateur *m.*	computer
Molière (Jean-Baptiste)	Molière (Jean-Baptiste)	oreille *f.*	ear
		osseux	bony
mon *f.*	my	où	where
moniteur *m.*	monitor	ours *m.*	bear
montagne (à la montagne)	in the mountains		
		P	
montre *f.*	watch	pain *m.*	bread
mots croisés *m. pl.*	crosswords	palmier *m.*	palm tree
mou	soft	pantalon *m.*	pants, trousers
mouette *f.*	seagull	parcmètre *m.*	parking meter
mouillé	wet	pare-brise *m.*	windshield
mouton *m.*	sheep	pare-chocs *m.*	bumper
mûr	ripe	partais (je)	I was leaving
musclé, musculaire	muscular	participes	participles
musée *m.*	museum	partirait (elle)	she would leave
musicien *m.*	musician	Pascal (Blaise)	Pascal (Blaise)
		passage souterrain *m.*	underpass
N		passe-temps *m.*	hobby
nappe *f.*	tablecloth	patient	patient
naugeux	cloudy	patinoire *f.*	rink
nausée *f.*	nausea	pause-café *f.*	coffee break
naviguer	to navigate	pêche *f.*	peach
neige (il)	(it is) snowing	pendule *f.*	clock
nerveux	nervous		

pensée f.	pansy
perdrais (tu)	you would lose
père m.	father
permanente f.	permanent wave
personne f.	person
petit	small, short
petits pains m. pl.	buns
peuple m.	populace, people
peut (il)	he can
Peut-être!	Maybe!
phares m. pl.	headlights
pied m.	foot
pigeon m.	pigeon
pilote m.	pilot
pin m.	pine tree
pingouin f.	penguin
piscine f.	swimming pool
piste f.	ski slope
plafond m.	ceiling
pleut (il)	(it is) raining
plombage m.	filling
plombier m.	plumber
plumes f. pl.	feathers
pluriel	plural
pneu m.	tire
poire f.	pear
poirier m.	pear tree
policier m.	police
pomme f.	apple
pomme de terre f.	potato
pommier m.	apple tree
pompier m.	firefighter
pont m.	bridge
portable m.	laptop
porte f.	door
portefeuille m.	wallet
portion f.	serving
possessifs	possessives
poule f.	hen
pourboire m.	tip
pour moi	for me
pourquoi	why
pourrais (je)	I could

pouvait (il)	he was able to, he could
premier	first
prendre	to have (to take)
prendre de l'exercice	to exercise, to work out
prennent (elles)	they take
present m.	present
professeur m.	professor
programme m.	program
prune f.	plum
pu	could, was able to
pudding m.	pudding
pullover m.	sweater
purée de pommes de terre f.	mashed potatoes
puzzle m.	jigsaw puzzle

Q

quand	when
quartier m.	district
quatre-vingts	eighty
que	what, that, which
quenotte f.	tooth (colloquial)
qu'est-ce que	what
qu'est-ce qui	who
qui	who, whom, that, which
quinzième	fifteenth
quoi	what

R

racine f.	root
radio f.	radio
radis m.	radish
raisins f. pl.	grapes
réanimation f.	intensive care
réception f.	front desk
recevons (nous)	we receive
recevront (ils)	they will receive
regarderiez (vous)	you would look at
regardez (vous)	you look at
règle f.	ruler

régulier	regular
Renoir (Jean)	Renoir (Jean)
Renoir (Pierre-Auguste)	Renoir (Pierre-Auguste)
renverser	to spill
renvoyer	to fire
répondraient (ils)	they would answer
réseau *m.*	network
réservation *f.*	reservation
restaurant *m.*	restaurant
retraite *f.*	retirement
réussira (il)	he will succeed
robe *f.*	dress
robinet *m.*	faucet
Rodin (François-Auguste)	Rodin (François-Auguste)
rompions (nous)	we were breaking
rompu	broken
rond	round
rose	pink
rôti *m.*	roast, roasted
rouge	red
rougiras (tu)	you will turn red
route *f.*	road
rude	rude, rough
rue *f.*	street
ruelle *f.*	alley

S

sa *f.*	his/her
salade de fruit	fruit salad
salaire *m.*	salary
salami *m.*	salami
salé	salty
salle *f.*	hospital ward
salle à manger *f.*	dining room
salle de bains *f.*	bathroom
salle de séjour *f.*	living room
sandale *f.*	sandal
sandwich *m.*	sandwich
sapin *m.*	fir tree
sardines *f. pl.*	sardines
saumon *m.*	salmon

sauras (tu)	you will know
sec	dry
séchoir *m.*	dryer
semelle *f.*	sole
sentir	to taste
serai (je)	I will be
serre *f.*	greenhouse
servaient (ils)	they were serving
serveur *m.*	server
serveuse *f.*	waitress
serviettes *f. pl.*	towels
servir	to serve
ses *m. pl.*	her
siège *m.*	seat
S'il vous plaît!	Please!
sincère	sincere
singe *m.*	monkey
sitcom *f.*	sitcom
site *m.*	website
ski *m.*	skiing
soap-opéra *m.*	soap opera
société *f.*	company
soeur *f.*	sister
soif *f.*	thirst
soixante-dix	seventy
sol *m.*	floor
soleil (il fait du …)	sunny (it is …)
sommes (nous)	we are
son *f.*	her
sortent (ils)	they leave
souris *f.*	mouse
sous l'eau	underwater
souvent	often
spaghetti *m. pl.*	spaghetti
stade *m.*	stadium
steward *m.*	male flight attendant
stylo *m.*	pen
su	knew
surfer	to surf
sur la table	on the table
syndicat *m.*	labor union

T

ta *f.*	your
table *f.*	table
tailleur *m.*	tailor
talon *m.*	heel
tante *f.*	aunt
tasse *f.*	cup
télécarte *f.*	phone card
télécommande *f.*	remote control
téléphoner	to phone
téléviseur *m.*	television set
tennis *m.*	tennis
terrain *m.*	playing field
tête *f.*	head
théière *f.*	teapot
tiers (un tiers)	one third
tomate *f.*	tomato
toujours	always
tousser	to cough
travailler	to work
travaux *m. pl.*	works
tribunal *m.*	courthouse
tristesse *f.*	sadness
trois cents	three hundred
trombone *m.*	paper clip
trottoir *m.*	sidewalk
tulipe *f.*	tulip

U

une heure cinq	five past one
une heure et demi	half past one

V

université *f.*	university
urgence *f.*	emergency
vacances *f. pl.*	vacation
vache *f.*	cow
vendra (elle)	she will sell
vendrions (nous)	we would sell
vent (il fait du …)	windy (it is …)
vernis à ongles *m.*	nail polish
verre *m.*	drinking glass
verser	to pour
vert	green
vertiges *m. pl.*	dizziness
veste *f.*	jacket
vidéo *f.*	video/DVD player
vieux *m. pl.*	old men
vin *m.*	wine
vingt-et-unième	twenty-first
violet	purple
violette *f.*	violet
vive *f.*	lively
volant *m.*	steering wheel
voleur *m.*	thief
votre *m.*	your

Y, Z

yeux *m. pl.*	eyes
zoo *m.*	zoo